Post Traumatic School Disorder

Empowerment Strategies for African American Males

Dr. William "Flip" Clay

Copyright © 2011 Dr. William "Flip" Clay
All rights reserved.

ISBN: 1463727623
ISBN-13: 9781463727628

Contents

Dedication v
Acknowledgments vii
Preface ix
Introduction xv
1. Post Traumatic Stress Disorder 1
2. Post Traumatic School Disorder 5
3. The Demystification of Black Males
   (Hoodwinked-Bamboozled) 13
4. Dear Mother (Ping Pong Parenting) 23
5. Where Is My Father? (Songs from the Soul) 33
6. Post Traumatic School Disorder Treatment 41
7. Empowerment Program
   (Action, Attitude, Accountability) 49
8. Thinking Outside the Box
   (Social Media Counseling) 61
9. Conclusion 85
Appendix A: The Alphabet of Life 87
Appendix B: Parental Involvement
Strategies for Teachers and Administrators 89
Appendix C: Parenting Strategies 91

Appendix D: Empowering Resources 93
Appendix E: Teacher Counselor 95
Appendix F: Don't Let Go
    (Dedicated to single mothers) 97
About the Author 99
References 101

Dedication

This book is dedicated to all the parents, youth care workers, educators, counselors, mentors, and people helping Yahweh's children. All praises to Yahshua!

Jeremiah 29:11: "'For I know the plans I have for you,' declares the LORD, 'plans to prosper you and not to harm you, plans to give you hope and a future.'"

Acknowlegements

I'd like to say thank you to my family, friends, colleagues, and professors. To the esteemed Dr. Sonya Ford, I am honored to have received your patience and guidance. I couldn't have done this without your support. To Erik Cork, my mentor since 2004, your leadership in directing my steps has enhanced my professional career. To Marcus Wiley, "Bishop Secular" of the Yolanda Adams morning show, you're a true inspiration. To Dr. Tiffany Bowling, you're a true friend. To Dr. Max Ragland, thanks for all your support and encouragement. To Dr. Latasha Blanding, we made it through together! To the Prince George's County Professional School Counselors in Prince George's County Maryland, thanks for all you do for children.

Also, thanks to Renee Nash WHUR 96.3; you have always supported my passion for children. To my editor, Dawn Herring of Always Write, thanks for your extraordinary work. I would further like to thank Reverend Dr. Howard Willis Jr. of Greater Mt. Pisgah Baptist Church in Washington, DC. It's been a blessed friendship. Special thanks to my anointed pastors, Reverend Dr. Grainger Browning, Jr. and Reverend Dr. Jo Ann Browning of Ebenezer African Methodist Episcopal Church (A.M.E.) in Fort Washington, Maryland. You both are the essence of man and woman. A special shout out goes to my Ebenezer A.M.E. church family. In addition, I would like to thank the Beyond the Walls ministry of Ebenezer A.M.E.

I would like to thank all the educators standing on the wall. Thanks also to my Blue and White family, Phi Beta Sigma Fraternity and Zeta Phi Beta Sorority Incorporated. I would like to say a special thank you to my deceased mother, Annie Mae Clay, for her unconditional love and support and her unceasing challenge to me: "promise me you will make something of yourself." To my sister Carmen Clay, I appreciate your love and support. To my father, William H. Clay Sr., thanks for your unconditional love. Finally, I give honor and glory to Yahweh (God).

Preface

I can recall my first job after completing my master's degree. I completed college in December and was hired the following January to work in a predominately White school district in Northern Virginia as an elementary school counselor. As an elementary school counselor, I felt like I could make a difference because of what I went through as a child. I was an itinerate counselor assisting the school-based counselors with their duties. I was assigned to four schools. I loved the idea of going to four different schools and meeting the various parents, students, and teachers. It seemed to me every teacher wanted me to speak with all the boys, especially Black boys. I felt like a star. My success came from the fact that I was energetic, crazy, creative, down to earth, funny, engaging, and I spoke to kids on their level. I've always had a passion for helping children, especially Black boys. Teachers would always ask, "What did you say to them? They have changed their behavior!" I didn't do anything special, just be myself. My first year was a great learning experience. I learned to deal with those teachers, parents, and others who didn't like me because of the color of my skin, while taking pleasure in interacting with those who loved me because I loved children.

I can recall my first real eye-opener as a counselor. A teacher, I'll call her Ms. K, stated, "Mr. Clay, I really need to speak with you about one of my students."

I said, "Okay, what's wrong?"

"Well, we were drawing snowman pictures, and one of my students asked for his picture back because he wanted to put snowflakes on it."

I was confused. "What's wrong with snowflakes?" I asked.

"Well, he put the snowflakes on the chest of the snowman and called them boobies." She then told me, "I'm also concerned because he has a girlfriend in the classroom."

I stood there thinking, *He's five. What does he know about boobies and girlfriends?* I had to figure out how I was going to talk to this child about snowflake boobies on a snowman. I always kept magazines around because pictures were a good conversation point for kids. As I went through my magazines, I found the *Sports Illustrated* swimsuit magazine. I brought the boy in and asked him to look through the magazine and tell me which pictures he liked. I watched him turn the pages, and when he saw those women in the swimsuits, his eyes widened. I asked, "Why do you like those pictures so much?"

He said, "Because my mommy has snowflakes. We take showers, and we watch movies together." He continued, "And Ms. K's snowflakes are larger than Ms. W's snowflakes."

"How do you know?" I asked.

He replied, "Because me and my two friends call them to the table, and when they come to the table, we look at them when they bend over to help us."

"Okay," I answered slowly. I moved on to the next question. "So I heard you have a girlfriend?"

"Yes, I have two girlfriends. One girl is real quiet, but the other one talks back to her mom a lot. The quiet one is in my class."

"How do you know the other girl talks back to her mom?"

"I go over her house and stay overnight and play in the backyard. We kiss in the backyard, but don't tell my parents."

I then asked, "What kind of movies do you watch with your mommy?"

He said, "Snowflake movies."

I said okay were going back to class. As we walked back to class, I was in shock. I spoke with Ms. K, and she was shocked as well. She told me that it explained why they kept calling Ms. W (the teacher assistant) and her to their table.

Next, I had to talk to the parents. How was I going to tell a stay-at-home mother her son told me they watched snowflake movies and took showers together? Well, I explained the story to the mother, and she told me that, yes, they did take showers together, and when he was younger, they would watch movies as a family, but she never thought he was really paying attention because he was two years old at the time. I explained that kids are very curious and asked her to please be careful what she did in front of her children. After that incident, I knew school counseling was my calling.

During my tenure in that Virginia school system, I met some beautiful people. I'll never forget Brenda Herman, a White school counselor who was the spitting image of me. She loved the children, and everything she did exemplified enthusiasm, energy, love, and passion. I enjoyed going to her school, and it gave me the opportunity to see firsthand a young White female working with Black boys. I'll also always remember Linda Falden, a Black school counselor who adopted me as a son. She would always give me words of encouragement. During my tenure in Northern Virginia, there were people who thought I was too "urban." I was teaching guidance lessons using rap, rhymes, and rhythms. I would say things to children in their language, and several people didn't approve of my techniques. I never let that stop me from helping the children. I wanted kids to learn about proper behavior in an engaging manner. As time progressed, I started building a better rapport with all the children. Several of the children would call me "daddy." I never had a problem with it because I understood why they did it; growing up, my father didn't live in my house, just like many of theirs. A lot of people thought it wasn't right, though, so I had to start telling the kids to stop. I can recall the look on the Black kids' faces when I told them not to call me daddy; it was heartbreaking. The White kids very seldom said it, but every now and then it did occur. I can recall one particular Friday when I was on bus duty. On bus duty days, the kids would always run up and give me hugs. On this particular day, there was a White girl and a Black girl waiting to say goodbye. The White girl said, "Bye, Daddy."

The Black girl told her, "He is not your father!"

The White girl replied, "In God's eyes, he is."

When she said that, time froze for me. I went to my office and tried to fight the tears. Here was a child who didn't see color, only the Godly love I had for children.

Preface

After a short tenure in that school district, I was told they weren't going to offer me another contract. Even my principal was surprised. He told me, "You're a real good counselor, Mr. Clay. I hate to lose you." I was upset that the school district didn't offer me another contract, but sometimes Yahweh allows us to "go through to get to." As a result, I was hired by Prince George's County Public Schools in Prince George's County, Maryland, a school district that was predominately Black.

At that point, based on my experience, I decided to take counseling Black boys to another level. I started forming empowerment programs among my Black boy population. The programs were life-changing. I was shocked that people were so accepting compared to my last school district. The feedback from the parents was extraordinary. From there, I started my own educational consulting practice. I began presenting at local conferences, schools, churches, and community agencies.

I can recall speaking at my first national conference in Atlanta, Georgia. My mentor, Erik Cork, introduced me at the National Association of Black School Educators national conference. There were over 150 people in the room, and I was nervous; people from all over the country were there to hear me. I was the bomb!

As time progressed, my empowerment program went to yet another level. I could see the lives of Black boys changing daily. Now ten years later, I know it's time to share these techniques with parents, teachers, counselors, community service workers, and other people working with children or youth in any capacity.

Introduction

One of the major problems facing the educational system in the United States is the widespread inequity in educational achievement and opportunity across ethnic and socioeconomic groups. On a variety of measures, such as standardized tests, advanced placement tests, and achievement tests, minorities, especially African American boys, have lower levels of achievement. African American boys in the school system are a prime example of a marginalized group of students who are not excelling to their capacity. As a result, the school counseling profession has been under pressure to develop strategies to close the achievement gap.

At the inception of school counseling back in the early 1900s, school counselors were vital in vocational guidance; as the profession expanded, counselors began to examine school counseling from a cognitive perspective (*1*). The cognitive approach allowed professional school counselors to examine school counseling from an individual perspective. Niebuhr, Niebuhr, and Cleveland (*2*) noted that by the late 1990s, school counselors faced a wider range of responsibilities and opportunities to offer services to a diverse population of students. As a result, school counselors were unable to address some of the educational inequalities of minority students throughout the United States (*3*).

According to Kunjufu (4), African Americans represent 17% of the school population but constitute over 30% of the children placed in special education. Furthermore, African American boys make up over 75% of the students placed in special education (5). Whether the blame is extrinsic or intrinsic, at the heart of the counseling process lays the responsibility of the professional school counselor to provide the necessary services to enhance student achievement. The American School Counselors Association (ASCA) began to address this challenge of improving academic achievement by asking how students are different because of what school counselors do. As a result, the ASCA created a national model (6), a framework for school counselor programs across the country. The ASCA national model's focus is to bridge counseling and academic achievement via systemic and collaborative efforts between counselors, teachers, administrators, parents, and students (3).

As I wrote this book, I started to ask myself what role my school counselor played in my life. I can recall growing up in public schools, and I could never sit still. I was the average student maintaining A's, B's, and C's in elementary school. School was okay, but I really liked my teacher, Ms. Lee. She was a beautiful White woman with long black hair. I loved seeing her pretty face and couldn't wait to get a hug from her. Even though I got on her nerves, her words of encouragement meant the world to me. I lived at home with my father, mother, and sister. My house was nice! I had my own bedroom and playroom in the basement. My friends would come over and play at my house because of my basement.

Introduction

My friend Michael lived next door. His father didn't live with him, but we seldom talked about it. When we did talk about it, he would say that he wished his father lived with him. He would always tell me how lucky I was to have both parents. What Michael didn't know was that my parents argued and screamed a lot. I never told anyone at school about my problems because my father always taught me to be tough and not show any emotions. Plus, back then, I thought counselors didn't focus on emotional stuff. My parents finally separated, and I went from living in a nice neighborhood to living in the "hood." I was devastated. Finally, years later, my parents divorced. My mom worked her butt off trying to make it through the days. I went to school in pain, smiling on the outside but sad within. We moved again about two years later, and my mother was diagnosed with cancer around my first year in middle school. I can recall her teaching me how to cook, clean, and be responsible. She told me one day I would have to take care of her. So along with the divorce, I was dealing with my mother's sickness. My grades started dropping, but I didn't care because I was worried about my mother. I was in pain and didn't understand why my father never came by to see us. My grandmother was always there for me, and she was the only one I really talked to about my problems. I had a school counselor, but I was ashamed to talk about what I was feeling. See, I was taught at an early age that little boys don't show their emotions. As time passed, my mother became worse. I remember one day sitting at the kitchen table and my mother said something I would never forget.

"You know I'm sick, but promise me two things," she said.

I asked, "What, Mommy?"

"Promise me you will make something of yourself, and never treat a women like your father treated me."

Not long after that, the doctor told us that my mother only had six months to live. The cancer was eating up her body, and every night she would moan in pain. I was going to school and getting up eight to ten times a night to ease her pain. Sometimes, I would give her medication or water. This actually went on for about a year. I was tired, in pain, and very stressed, but I never felt comfortable talking to my school counselor. After a while, my mother got so bad that she couldn't walk, so I would pick her up and take her to the bathroom. On one particular night, I was really tired, and as I carried her into the bathroom, I accidently dropped her. Luckily, the wall caught her because it was right next to the toilet. I can still see the expression on her face. The next day, I tried to be cool, but deep down I was an emotional train wreck.

After my mother died, I really wanted to talk to my school counselor, but I thought counselors didn't talk to kids about their families. I found out I was wrong. I finally decided to open up and talk to my school counselor, and the burden of several years was finally unleashed. I'm thankful I had a school counselor to help me deal with my emotions. Sometimes I wonder where I would be without my school counselor. Other than my school counselor, my grandmother was my only resource.

Introduction

I moved in with my grandma when my mother died. I saw my father sometimes, but he never really spent time with me. My father would bring my money, but I wanted his presence, not his presents. I always wondered, *What did I do?* After my mother died, I started seeking guidance and direction. I was seeking male role models. There was one in particular who really guided me without his knowledge. It was my cousin, Benjamin Brown Jr. He attended Elizabeth City State College, played basketball, and pledged Alpha Phi Omega. He would come home from college and tell me all kinds of stories. There was also Roland Holloway, who attended Virginia Union University and pledged Kappa Alpha Psi. I became motivated to be just like them. They became my fathers away from home.

I made it out of high school with C's and D's. After graduating, I worked for a couple of years and then went to Charleston, WV Job Corps. During my tenure in Charleston Job Corps, I was awarded student of the year. From there, I went to West Virginia State College. My dad would sometimes send me money while I was in college. One particular day he went to the post office to send me ten dollars (my father was tight on a dollar), but the lady accidently put one hundred dollars on the money order. When I got that money order, I was shocked; to this day, he doesn't know I know the truth, but my sister told me what happened. My father said I deserved the money.

College allowed me to clear my mind, but I can recall that at the beginning of the semester when the kids were returning to school, I didn't like it because my father wasn't there. I was older but still thought about my childhood. I was a grown man but was still dealing with the same emotional problems I had as a child. I thank Yahweh my school counselor was there for me, which I know started the healing process. Finally, I graduated from West Virginia State College. From there, I attended Virginia State University, where I pledged Phi Beta Sigma fraternity. I graduated and began working as an elementary school counselor. I remember my father saying, "Man, I'm surprised you made it further than your sister." I understood she was a daddy's girl.

After several years of working in the profession, I began to heal from my childhood. As I shared my story with boys, especially Black boys, I was set free. Several years down the road, I found myself enrolled in a doctoral degree program. Four rough years later, I recalled the words of my mother: "Promise me you'll make something of yourself, and never treat a woman like your father treated me." On December 15, 2010, I became Dr. William Clay. I thank Yahweh for my mother's words of wisdom, for my grandmother, Edith Mae Marsh, for my immediate family members who were role models, for my father's ability to admit his mistakes and at least be present in some fashion, and for the fact that I had a school counselor with whom I could share my burden.

The role school counselors play in the lives of children is vital to their success, especially Black boys, who are considered at risk. Counselors today serve as grandfathers, grandmothers, fathers, and mothers. It's the role of the professional school counselors to teach boys, especially young Black boys, to share their emotions.

Introduction

It's their duty to share with them strategies to empower them into manhood. It's their role to be the third ear, the ear that could be the difference between life and death, doing drugs, dropping out of school, getting pregnant, robbing someone, cheating on a test, fighting a teacher, accepting family members, dealing with divorce, and finally making the right choices. It's their job to empower all students, especially Black boys, and to tell them that excellence is embedded within them through the likes of Ben Carson, Carter G. Woodson, Garrett Morgan, Eli Whitney, Charles Drew, Benjamin Baneker, Lewis Latimer, Malcolm X, Martin Luther King Jr., and President Barack Obama. As I reflect on my position as a professional school counselor, the words of Na'im Akbar (7) come to mind: "When problems are analyzed with the essential focus on the negative, then the solutions will invariably be reactions rather than actions. The answer to helping African American boys lies in taking a holistic approach to solving their mental, social, and academic needs." Such holistic thinking is difficult for some educators who are deeply entrenched in not utilizing school counselors according to the ASCA national model. It is hoped that school counselors, educators, parents, and mentors will use this book to develop the social, emotional, and academic levels of all students, especially Black boys.

Chapter 1
Post-Traumatic Stress Disorder

Proverb: An intelligent enemy is better than a stupid friend.

Post-Traumatic Stress Disorder (PTSD) is described in the *Diagnostic and Statistical Manual of Mental Disorders* (8). The latest version of the *Diagnostic Statistical Manual* is the fourth edition (DSM-IV). The DSM-IV is the primary tool used by mental health clinicians. The essential feature of PTSD is the development of characteristic symptoms following exposure to an extreme traumatic stressor involving direct personal experience of an event that incudes actual or threatened death or serious injury, or some other threat to one's physical integrity; or witnessing an event that involves death, injury, or a threat to the physical integrity of another person; or learning about unexpected or violent death, serious harm, or threat of death or injury experienced by a family member or other close associate (Criterion A1). Using this description, 400 years of slavery is a good example. The person's response to the event must involve intense fear, helplessness, or horror (or in children, the response must involve disorganized or agitated behavior; Criterion A2). The slaves shared various stories of intense fear. The characteristic symptoms resulting from the exposure to the extreme trauma include persistent re-experiencing of the traumatic event (Criterion B). Once slaves were brought to America, they continued to experience slavery. Next is the persistent avoidance of stimuli associated with the trauma and numbing of general responsiveness (Criterion C), and finally, persistent symptoms of increased arousal (Criterion D). I can recall talking with several African Americans who became very agitated and said we must stop using slavery as an excuse. The full symptom picture must be present for more than one month (Criterion E), and the disturbance must cause clinically significant distress or impairment in social, occupational, or other important areas of functioning (Criterion F). The African Holocaust and Jim Crow were present for over 400 years, and if you look at the mental condition of some African American males, especially Black boys, in America today, there is significant distress or impairment in social and occupational areas of functioning.

The DSM-IV specifiers include the following:

- Acute: This specifier should be used when the duration of symptoms is less than three months.
- Chronic: This specifier should be used when the symptoms last three months or longer.
- With delayed onset: This specifier indicates that at least six months have passed between the traumatic event and the onset of the symptoms.

There are associated features and disorders with PTSD. However, the DSM-IV does not know to what extent these disorders precede or follow the onset of

PTSD (8). With that said, some people believe that you can't associate slavery and Jim Crow with Black boys in the school system. I respect their opinion; however, when American soldiers fight in wars, they seek treatment upon return because of the trauma they experienced. Any competent clinician or counselor knows that when you don't treat a person or group of people who've experienced trauma, there will be generational ramifications. In my experience as a school counselor, when I share with Black children the African Holocaust (slavery), their whole demeanor changes. They start to appreciate what their ancestors went through. If we are serious about closing the achievement gap, we must begin to expose all Black children, especially Black boys, to their true history.

Chapter 2
Post-Traumatic School Disorder

Proverb: A tree is known by its fruit.

It is no secret that the institution of slavery impacts education today. Since the institution of slavery, education has represented the practice of freedom (9) for African Americans in the United States. The educational accomplishments of countless members of the Black community represent a rejection of the dominant societal narrative that says African Americans have a history of underperformance in America's public schools (10). In fact, the counter narrative of Black children's school success serves to motivate many students who might otherwise internalize the myth of Black intellectual inferiority and experience consistent academic underperformance. The educational struggles endured and advancements made by Blacks as a group since slavery are a testament to a prevailing collective commitment to developing and maintaining positive racial and achievement-oriented identities in a society where an individual's racial group membership often renders one as less-than, subordinate, and/or invisible. Thus, despite living in a culture in which being Black is often perceived as being academically and intellectually inferior by the larger society (11), the counter narrative of Black school success highlights people's continued understanding of the utility of schooling as a viable option for positive life outcomes.

From the earliest times in American history, the U.S. educational system mandated separate schools for children based solely on race. Court cases against segregated schools have been documented as far back as 1849. In 1861, the Civil War was fought, dividing the country along the lines of who should receive full rights and privileges under the U.S. Constitution. This conflict centered around the status of people of African descent who had been brought to America as slave labor. Those who would end the practice of slavery prevailed. Yet, in spite of the end of the Civil War in 1865, the inclusion of African Americans as full citizens required amending the U.S. Constitution. As a result, the Civil War was followed by the enactment of the 13th Amendment, which was ratified in 1865 and abolished slavery; the 14th Amendment, which was ratified in 1868 and conferred citizenship on the formerly enslaved people of African descent and bestowed equal protection under the law; and the 15th Amendment, ratified in 1870, which affirmed that the right of U.S. citizens to vote cannot be denied or abridged on account of race. In spite of the mandates outlined in the newly amended U.S. Constitution, freedom and equal rights were not readily bestowed upon Blacks. Throughout this period, education was withheld from people of African descent. In some states, it was against the law for this segment of the population to learn to read and write. Tremulous disappointment and disillusionment stirred African American people to continue to challenge this system of segregation. As a result, the *Brown v. Board of Education* court case was heard after an African American student was denied the right to attend an all-White school seven blocks from her home.

Although all public schools were supposed to be equal, most African American schools were inferior to White schools. In many instances, the schools for African American children were substandard facilities with out-of-date textbooks and insufficient supplies. The *Brown* decision initiated educational reform throughout the United States and was a catalyst in launching the modern Civil Rights Movement. However, bringing about change proved difficult. After the *Brown v. Board of Education* decision, schools with African American children remained inferior (*12*). Four hundred years later, one thing that hasn't changed much is the underachievement of African American males at all levels. We must ask ourselves, "Why are Black boys still performing below their White counterparts?"

Educational and psychological research has long noted that students of African descent tend to experience poor academic outcomes relative to White students (*4*). There have been numerous explanations in literature for these trends, including differences in cognitive style, aversion to intellectual competition, teaching styles, language barriers, genetics, and general cultural differences (*13*). According to Ogbu (*14*), several theories examine these trends. For example, cultural-ecological theory explores how culture, identity, and societal forces impact the educational outcomes of minority groups. Culture-centered theory (CCT) examines the use of students' cultural backgrounds as a point of reference for preparing those students academically and socially. Finally, critical race theory (CRT) explores the sociopolitical consequences of race in educational settings from a progressive legal perspective. While these theories are promising in providing insight into the experiences of Black youth, none of them comprehensively capture the intragroup differences and identity processes that affect Black youth in all social and educational settings. For example, if cultural differences are the culprit, why do children who migrate from cultures drastically different from the majority culture often do better academically than African American boys who come from families and communities with cultures that are arguably more similar to those of the majority culture (*15*)?

One explanation, the cultural dissonance explanation, holds that White educators do not understand the culture of African American children and therefore misinterpret their behavior and impose sanctions more frequently or more harshly on African American children, leading to conflict and disaffection with school. As a result, most African American children in public schools are unsuccessful, and then they start to suffer from low self-esteem, especially if the curriculum materials do not reflect either their culture or interests (*7*). Another theory, closely aligned with cultural dissonance, is that educators do not understand the learning styles of African American children, and, therefore, the teaching and learning experiences of African American children are negatively affected (*13*). Akbar (*7*) argued that for

African American children to succeed, it becomes necessary for them to reject their own identities and act White, while DuBois (*16*) discussed the concept of employing double consciousness, which means always looking at the world from the eyes of White people. Others have sought explanations in the children themselves, arguing certain racial groups are intellectually inferior to others and that African American children misbehave, causing them to justifiably be placed in lower academic percentiles. But the explanation that has been widely put forward by parents, educators, pastors, and counselors is that structural, institutional, and individual racism are the causes of low academic achievement among African Americans boys (*7*). Consequently, some other cultural differences theorists have argued that the disproportionate school failure of African American boys can be attributed at best to the mismatch between the home culture and school culture. The assumption is that the culture of the school is the dominant culture, the culture of mainstream White America (*17*). Albert Bandura's Social Learning Theory argues that behaviors are learned observationally through modeling, and that environment, behavior, and reciprocal interaction play a role in what students learn (*18*). Though many theorists have developed responses to this phenomenon, there still remains a large gap in academic achievement; thus, the exploration of other possible causes and solutions is necessary.

In essence, Post-Traumatic School Disorder is a non-diagnosed emotional disorder that exemplifies itself in the behaviors of African American boys in education today as a result of slavery, lack of civil rights, Jim Crow, Jane Crow, and forced integration. Like Post-Traumatic Stress Disorder, Post-Traumatic School Disorder has clearly defined criteria:

- Criterion 1: lazy, unfocused, angry, irritable, can't sit still, mischievous.
- Criterion 2: depressed, guilty, aggressive, confused, agitated, frustrated.
- Criterion 3: attention-seeking, outspoken, rebellious, low self-esteem.
- Criterion 4: identity crisis, violent, disrespectful, manipulative.

Specifiers include the following:

- Acute: During this phase in school, boys, especially Black boys, are reprimanded and misdiagnosed for behaviors.
- Chronic: During this phase in school, they are suspended, expelled, and eventually drop out.
- Delayed onset: During this phase in school, they are passed along just to get them out of the school system.

In my role as a consultant, I've been blessed to converse with numerous teachers about Black boys. In my role as a professional school counselor, I've seen firsthand the plight of Black boys. A majority of teachers, educators, and parents have similar concerns. They state that Black boys are angry, frustrated, unfocused, irritable, lazy, and can't sit still (Criterion 1). As a professional school counselor, I've personally observed the following emotions: blame, guilt, anger, anxiety, depression, aggression, avoidance, confusion, and agitation (Criterion 1 and 2). I can recall numerous meetings with teachers who stated, "I think he has ADD/ADHD." I would often cringe because deep down, I knew that likely wasn't the problem. I would ask myself, "If I had survived slavery and Jim Crow, if I had been forced to attend schools where I wasn't wanted, how would I behave?" The problem also lies in the curriculum, self-identity, self-esteem, teacher perception and expectations, teaching styles, school culture, parental involvement, time on task, counselor advocacy, and, as discussed below, emotional constipation and emotional incarceration.

There are two phases of Post-Traumatic School Disorder that Black boys exemplify in school. The first behavior is emotional constipation. This occurs from the age of five to about fourteen. During this phase, some Black boys exhibit behaviors that are contrary to school norms. For instance, they can't sit still and are talkative and mischievous (Criterion 1); they seem angry, frustrated, unfocused, and unemotional (Criterion 1 and 2); and they are outspoken, seek attention, and exhibit low self-esteem (Criterion 3). The second behavior is emotional incarceration. This occurs between the ages of fourteen and nineteen. During this time period, some Black boys develop negative attitudes toward school, teachers, parents, society, and themselves. They exemplify aggression and depression, are easily provoked, experience identity crisis, and are prone to violence (Criterion 4). The only reason they go to school is to socialize. They skip class, walk the halls, use profanity, disrespect females, manipulate their parents, disrespect authority, use drugs, disrespect themselves, join gangs, walk around with their pants sagging, and become less concerned about life and education. They reinforce society's false image of African American males.

Educators, counselors, parents, and students must be aware of the existence of Post-Traumatic School Disorder and the symptoms that some African American males may exhibit if we are serious about closing the achievement gap.

Chapter 3

The Demystification of African American Males (Hoodwinked and Bamboozled)

Proverb: A fool is always right in his own eyes—no wonder he is a fool.

Research suggests that Black students' racial identity impacts academic achievement and school behaviors (*19*). Having a sense of self as a member of the Black community represents one protective factor or buffer that facilitates Black youths' development of positive achievement beliefs and subsequent academic adjustment (*20*). According to Oyserman, Gant, and Ager (*20*), a positive African American identity schema encompasses three aspects: (a) seeing oneself as a member of the racial group (i.e., connectedness); (b) being aware of stereotypes and limitations to one's present and future social and economic outcomes (i.e., awareness of racism); and (c) developing a perspective of self as succeeding as a racial group member (i.e., achievement as an African American). Under this framework, the aforementioned aspects provide what is necessary to acquire school success. Building upon this framework, researchers suggest that racial centrality (the degree to which an individual values race as a core part of his/her self-concept) is related to higher academic achievement ([21]). Racial centrality is similar to Oyserman et al.'s ([20]) notion of connectedness, in which Black adolescents describe a sense of self as part of Black family and kin networks. A sense of connectedness to the Black Community provides a sense of meaning and purpose.

The atrocities of slavery were treacherous. One example of an atrocity occurred when slaves were brought to the slave-breaking islands (Jamaica, Barbados, Cuba, etc.) and Caucasian slave enforcers would gather all the pregnant women, pick out ten women, and hang them by their feet. The overseer would take a machete and slice open the hanging women's abdomens, one by one, and the onlookers were forced to watch the unborn children fall out of the sliced women's wombs. Another atrocity involved cutting a child's body into pieces and forcing parents to watch as the child's mutilated body was fed to the hogs.

Furthermore, during the middle passage, slaves were brought to America in despicable traveling conditions. When families were brought to the ship, they were separated. The men who fastened the irons would take the children and throw them over the side of the ship into the water. The mothers would dive into the water to save their children. Once on board, slaves were chained together below the ship in what was called the slave galley. They didn't have enough room, not even as much as a man in his coffin, either in length or depth. They could not turn or shift with any degree of ease. Confine-

The Demystification

ment in this situation was so injurious that a slave could be in good health during the day yet be found dead in the morning. Slavery differed from country to country; however, slavery in America was cruel. There was a process called seasoning. This process consisted of strong men and women being emotionally broken, tortured, and stripped of their dignity. Slaves were taught to believe they were innately inferior and accepted slavery as their natural condition. The seasoning process for some Black boys starts in elementary school. As a result, they are labeled, reprimanded, and start to believe they are inferior.

It took months, years, even generations to break the spirits, but slave masters knew this was essential for slavery to survive. For example, to make slaves stand in fear, slave masters would (a) establish and maintain strict discipline; (b) implant in the slave a consciousness of personal inferiority; (c) awe the bondsman with a sense of the master's enormous power; (d) persuade the slave to take an interest in the master's enterprise and to accept his standards of good conduct; and (e) impress in the slave an utter sense of helplessness to create a habit of perfect dependence (22). Once the psychological torture altered a slave's behavior, when the slave feared more for his or her own survival than the survival of the group, the seasoning process was complete.

Each generation underwent a series of psychological and physical torture to make them stand in fear (23). Slaves were hung by their thumbs, beaten with a paddle, castrated, mutilated, decapitated, burned, chocked to death, bound, covered with molasses to attract biting insects, or left to blister in the burning sun. James Ball, a slave in the South, described the whip used on the plantation as follows:

> The lash is ten feet long, made of small strips of buckskin, tanned so as to be dry and hard, and plaited carefully and closely together, of a thickness, in the largest part, of a man's finger. At the farthest end of this thong is attached a cracker, nine inches in length, made of strong sewing silk, twisted and knotted, until it feels as firm as hardest twine. Once felt on bare flesh, the burning sting of the whip could never be forgotten. (cited in 24)

Another example was when the master would throw a woman into buck and whip her. He would then tie her hands together and strip her naked. Next, he would force her to squat down, and he would run a stick through behind her knees and in front of her elbows, so that her knees were up against her chest. Her hands were tied together in front of her shins. Explained one woman who underwent this treatment:

> The stick between my arms and my knees held me in a squat. That's what they called a buck. You couldn't stand up and you couldn't get your feet out. You couldn't do nothing but squat there and take what he put on. You couldn't move no way at all. Just try to. If you tried to, you would fall over on one side and have to stay there until you were turned over by him. I was whipped on

one side until there was blood and I was tore up. Then I was whipped on the other side till that was tore up. I got a big scar as the place my ol' mistress hit me. She took a bull whip once. The bull whip had a piece of iron in the handle of it and she got mad. She was so mad so she took the whip and hit me over the head with the butt end and blood flew. It ran all down my back and dripped my heels. (cited in *24*).

Slavery as a whole had no redeeming virtues for the enslaved. This was evident in a speech made by Willie Lynch, a British slave owner in the West Indies who was invited to the colony of Virginia in 1712 to teach his methods to slave owners there. The following excerpt is from that speech:

> Take the female and run a series of tests on her to see if she will submit to your desires willingly. Test her in every way, because she is the most important factor for good economics. If she shows any sign of resistance in submitting completely to your will, do not hesitate to use the bullwhip on her to extract that last bit of [b—] out of her. Take care not to kill her, for in doing so, you spoil good economics. When in complete submission, she will train her off springs in the early years to submit to labor when they become of age. (cited in *25*)

Morrow (25), in his analysis of Lynch's speech, reasoned the following:

Understanding is the best thing. Therefore, we shall go deeper into this area of the subject matter concerning what we have produced here in this breaking process of the female ni—. We have reversed the relationship; in her natural uncivilized state, she would have a strong dependency on the uncivilized ni— male, and she would have a limited protective tendency toward her independent male offspring and would raise male off springs to be dependent like her. Nature had provided for this type of balance. We reversed nature by burning and pulling a civilized ni— apart and bullwhipping the other to the point of death, all in her presence. By her being left alone, unprotected, with the male image destroyed, the ordeal caused her to move from her psychologically dependent state to a frozen, independent state. In this frozen, psychological state of independence, she will raise her male and female offspring in reversed roles. For fear of the young male's life, she will psychologically train him to be mentally weak and dependent, but physically strong. Because she has become psychologically independent, she will train her female off springs to be psychologically independent. As a result, you have a large percentage of black females successful in school and going to college. Whereas, most boys strive to be professional athletes. This is why black boys are emotionally constipated and incarcerated years after Willie Lynch.

According to Morrow, Lynch continued his speech as follows:

While Rome used cords of wood as crosses for standing human bodies along its highways in great numbers, you are here using the tree and the rope on occasions. I caught the whiff of a dead slave hanging from a tree, a couple miles back. You are not only losing valuable stock by hangings, you are having uprisings, slaves are running away, your crops are sometimes left in the fields too long for maximum profit, you suffer occasional fires, your animals are killed. Gentlemen, you know what your problems are; I do not need to elaborate. I am not here to enumerate your problems, I am here to introduce you to a method of solving them. In my bag here, I have a full proof method for controlling your black slaves. I guarantee every one of you that, if installed correctly, it will control the salves for at least three hundred years. My method is simple. Any member of your family or your overseer can use it. I have outlined a number of differences among the slaves; and I take these differences and make them bigger. I use fear, distrust and envy for control purposes. These methods have worked on my modest plantation in the West Indies and it will work throughout the South. Take this simple little list of differences and think about them. On top of my list is "age," but it's there only because it starts with an "a." The second is "color" or shade. There is intelligence, size, sex, attitude of owners, whether the slaves live in the valley, on a hill, East, West, North, South, have fine hair, course hair, or is tall or short. Now that you have a list of differences, I shall give you an outline of action, but before that, I shall assure you that distrust is stronger than trust and envy stronger than adulation, respect or admiration. The black slaves after receiving this indoctrination shall carry on and will become self-refueling and self-generating for hundreds of years, maybe thousands. Don't forget, you must pitch the old black male vs. the young black male, and the young black male against the old black male. You must use the dark skin slaves vs. the light skin slaves, and the light skin slaves vs. the dark skin slaves. You must use the female vs. the male, and the male vs. the female. You must also have white servants and overseers [who] distrust all blacks. Gentlemen, these kits are your keys to control. Use them. Have your wives and children use them, never miss an opportunity. (cited in 25)

As slavery continued, the public characterization of Blacks being intellectually inferior was dominant. The oppressor used every mode of communication to indoctrinate society into thinking Blacks were inferior. During that time period, Blacks were depicted as Chicken George, monkeys, coons, spooks, happy go lucky darky, blackface, and fiddlers. In the early 20th century, characters such as Stepin Fetchit, Fred Toones, and Willie Best were used to depict Blacks in a negative manner. Black and White minstrel shows were also used to depict Blacks in a negative manner. These shows traveled throughout the United States and became so popular they earned a primetime slot on television. The oppressor used books, television, education, doctors, and psychologists to portray Blacks as genetically inferior.

As illustrated previously, slavery was used to dehumanize and relegate Black slaves to nothing. How could this happen when Europeans knew Africa was the land kissed by the Gods? Africa is home of the Nile, the world's longest river; the Sahara, the world's largest desert; and Mount Kilimanjaro, one of the world's highest mountains. It's the home of Egypt, Timbuktu, civilization, commerce, medicine, mathematics, and knowledge. It is the birthplace of all life 4 million years ago. With that said, for African American students to achieve, they need to be sufficiently grounded in their identity as members of a racial caste group, such that they have a way to interpret and make sense of instances when they experience discrimination, especially in school. Once Black boys are taught they aren't "coons" but crusaders, that they are Imhotep not inhumane, and scholars not spooks, then they will no longer be hoodwinked and bamboozled. The truth will set them free academically and socially so they can become productive citizens.

Chapter 4

Dear Mama (Ping Pong Parenting)

Proverb: When a woman behaves like a woman, the man should behave like a man.

During slavery, Black children were denied the opportunity to develop to their fullest potential. At an early age, many were forced to work the cotton fields. Once in the fields, children were forced to work along with the adults, picking up to a hundred pounds a day. They were raped, beaten, and bullwhipped and were sold at the drop of a hat. In some instances, Black slave children slept on the floor beside the beds of White children, serving as helpmates. As a result, the parents didn't have sufficient opportunity to rear their own Black child because they were serving the needs of the master. Furthermore, after slavery was legally abolished, Black children were one of the most mistreated and neglected groups in American society (*26*). Four hundred years later, parents are still dealing with the effects of slavery on the family. As a result, one of the most consistent findings in educational research is the underachievement of African American boys at all levels of the educational pipeline (*27*).

Most social economic status and family structure effects on achievement are mediated by various family factors (28). The quality of parenting that children receive has a major effect on their development. Evidence from behavioral genetics research, as well as from experimental studies, shows that parenting practices have a major influence on children's development (29). Family risk factors, such as undereducated parents and marriage and family conflict, strongly influence children's risk of developing various forms of psychopathology (30). Specifically, a lack of warm, positive relationships with parents and insecure attachments coupled with harsh, inflexible, or inconsistent discipline practices or inadequate supervision strongly influence risk. This lack of attention is unfortunate because policy and interventions are more likely to succeed if they target family functioning as opposed to demographic factors (28). According to Kumpfer and Alvarado (31), most parents have the capacity to modify their parenting behavior in a way that is conducive to child development. The development of a positive self-image for Black boys starts with the acceptance that parents are the first primary educators. The parent-child relationship starts with parental care, which can be positive or negative. If a child wants to be an engineer, doctor, or accountant, there are schools for that; however, if one wants to learn how to be a better parent, there are few, if any, schools. As a result, the importance of child rearing and marriage is left to guesswork, trial and error, and whatever was picked up from one's own parents.

Values in the United States emphasize career and money, not family stability. These values have followed the changes in the economy, which has moved from agriculture to industrialism to post-industrialism. The family, in turn, has moved away from extended families to single-parent families, and the ill effects are felt most by African American women, given the imbalanced ratio of men to women. As a result, the future of Black boys lies in the hands of single mothers, grandmothers, stepmothers, fiancées, and foster mothers (5). According to research spanning from 1880 to 1960, the percentage of African American children living with a single parent held steady at around 30% (*32*). In 1920, 90% of African American youth had fathers in the household, and in 1960, 80% of African American youth had fathers in the household. However, in 2001, only 30% had fathers in the household (5). Since the 1960s, the percentage of African American children living with one parent has increased 63%, with 92% of these families headed by a woman (*33*).

The emotional trauma brought on slaves during the African Holocaust is still present today. As a result, the lack of success of Black boys in the family setting is increasing. The cause of lack of success varies from class, lack of role models, and parenting deficiencies to gender assumptions, policies, and procedures. There is an assumption that two-parent families are inherently better than one-parent families, and that single African American women somehow lack the skills to teach African America boys about manhood. Battle and Scott (*34*) stated that some studies suggest that single

African American females are an inadequate source of male socialization, which leads to poverty, drug abuse, school attendance problems, and low achievement. In contrast to the research emphasizing the negative impact on children raised in female-headed families, other recent research has not found a negative effect on children growing up in African American female-headed households, particularly when relevant factors such as family income were controlled (*35*). There is a fairly large body of research that challenges the assumption that boys raised by women are socially, culturally, and educationally deprived (*36*). The National Health Interview Survey Child Health Supplement (*37*) found that family structure in and of itself made no difference for adolescent academic, behavioral, or social emotional adjustment. Further research from the National Educational Longitudinal Study (NELS) found that economic resources available to the parents are much more important than the gender of the parents in the academic success of African American boys (*37*).

The question "what happened to the men?" has been asked by African American women because the fathers of African American boys have been missing. An effective strategy to destroy Black boys is to cause a divide between fathers and their children. During slavery, the master played the father slave against the mother slave. The slave master would degrade the male slave in front of the female slave. As slavery progressed, distrust in Black family became evident. Four hundred years later, the absence of fathers has led to the following problems: a lack of role models, a lack of money, the loneliness of the mother, and negative child-father perceptions.

In my experience as an elementary counselor, I can recall various counseling sessions related to the lack of fathers in the household. The boys would ask me questions like, "Does my father love me?" "Why does my mother talk about my father?" "Why don't my family live together?" Sometimes they would say, "My uncle stays at my house sometimes." I know "uncle" was code for boyfriend. I would also hear things like, "I stay with my mother during the weekdays, and on the weekends I'm with my father." Because of the lack of fathers in the lives of Black boys, it is imperative that single mothers use discretion and be selective as to whom they expose their children. I encourage single mothers to not use what I call "ping pong parenting strategies" to fulfill their wishes. Children are not ping pong balls. It's not right to bounce them back and forth and make them listen to negative comments by one parent about the other. I tell mothers all the time, "If you don't have anything good to say about his father, then don't say anything at all." Regardless of how a mother may feel, it's hard to stop a Black boy from loving his father. Based on my experience, mothers need to allow young Black boys to either develop or suffer the emotional imbalance that comes with a Black boy seeing his father. As long as there is no physical harm to the boy, allow him to make the decision about seeing his father based on how he feels about his father, not how you feel. His feelings shouldn't be a result of your comments.

Also, as a result of slavery, mothers today become very protective of boys. Over the years, I've noticed that mothers are quick to side with their sons. Kunjufu (*38*) explained that some mothers raise their daughters and love their sons, and that mothers often make daughters do homework, whereas they don't press their sons to do the same. According to Norment (*39*), Joyce Hamilton Berry, PhD, a clinical psychologist in the Washington, DC area, said the best way for a mother to teach her son to respect women is by demanding respect herself, such as demanding that he carry packages and groceries and that he open doors for her and other women. If a boy loves, respects, and reveres his mother, then most likely he will treat other women the same way. However, some mothers are so overprotective that the son becomes dependent, and this negatively affects his development. This dependency carries over into his relationships with women. If he can manipulate his mother, he will manipulate other women. Furthermore, this behavior negatively affects some aspects of him going into manhood. Mothers, please understand that you should not spoil or award Black boys when they don't deserve it. Raise them to be emotional beings so they will learn how to deal with expressing the pain that has hindered so many Black boys from becoming a man. If you don't, you are leading them right into the hands of destruction. Mothers, your son is not your friend. Spare the rod, spoil the child, and you will regret you ever did so.

I can recall working with a young boy named Trey whose parents were going through a divorce. He would always come by my office to discuss his feelings. One particular day, he caught me off guard when he said, "Mr. Clay, I love my dad and I love my mom, but my parents don't love me."

I asked, "Why would you say that?"

He replied, "Because every weekend I see my mother and she says bad things about my father."

Every Monday, he would come back to school feeling like the divorce was his fault. After listening to Trey, I started reflecting on my painful experience of divorce as a child. I can remember how my grades starting dropping. As I think about it today, it's the job of the parents to work out the differences between themselves without using the child as a ping pong ball. The problem is not single parenting, because it takes two to have children; however, being a single parent is different from single parenting. One allows for help while the other places all the responsibility on one person. In reality, children raised in a single-parent household have an 80% probability of raising children in a single-parent household (*40*). Furthermore, the adult male role in the family is essentially gone; however, if boys do not see and understand the role men should play in family life, they will have little appreciation and knowledge of how to interact in the future.

The reality of the matter is children need both of their parents to play a role in their academic success; however, with the issue of single parenting being so complex and rapidly increasing, it is imperative that professional school counselors handle this paradigm shift through using the ASCA national model for collecting information, examining societal circumstances, and collaborating with the students, parents, and teachers. The professional school counselor may use several parenting programs. A popular program is the Triple P Positive Parenting Program (Triple P; *41*) because it connects with the ASCA national model (*3*). The Triple P program was developed at the University of Queensland in Australia as a multilevel system of parenting intervention designed to improve the quality of parenting advice available to parents . A central goal of the Triple P is the development of an individual's capacity for self-regulation. Self-regulation is the process whereby individuals are taught skills to change their own behavior and become independent problem solvers in a broader social environment that supports parenting and family relationships. Another great aspect to the Triple P program is parental self-efficacy, which refers to a parent's belief that he or she can overcome or solve a specific parenting problem. Parents with high self-efficacy have more positive expectations that change is possible. Parents of children with behavior problems tend to have a lower task-specific self-efficacy in managing parenting responsibilities. The central goal of the intervention process is to foster greater confidence in daily parenting tasks. The use of self-management refers to the tools and skills that parents employ to enable them to change their parenting practices and become self-sufficient. These skills include self-monitoring, self-determination of performance criteria, and self-regulation of parenting strategies.

The goal of self-management is to help the parents select which aspect of their own and their child's behavior they wish to work on. Even though self-regulation and self-management tools are important aspects to the process, promoting problem solving is essential to the success of the Triple P program. Consequently, it is assumed that parents are active problem solvers and the interventions must equip parents to define problems, formulate options, develop parenting plans, execute the plans, evaluate the outcomes, and revise the plan as required. The Triple P training process must assist parents in generalizing their knowledge and skills so that they can apply principles and strategies to future problems at different points in a child's development.

The Triple P system aims to prevent severe behavioral, emotional, and developmental problems in children and adolescents by enhancing the knowledge, skills, and confidence of parents. This system incorporates five levels of intervention for parents of children from birth to age sixteen on a tiered continuum of increasing strength. The multilevel approach program is designed to create a family-friendly environment that supports parents in the task of raising their children. This process specifically targets the social context that influences the mass media, school systems, child care, religious organizations, and the broader political system. This multilevel strategy is designed to maximize efficiency, contain cost, avoid waste, and ensure the program has a wide reach in the community. One aspect of the program examines the five developmental periods from infancy to adolescence; within each developmental period, the reach of the intervention varies from very broad, targeting an entire population, to quite narrow, targeting high-risk students.

The following questions now arise: How can educators expect African American boys to excel academically when they do not feel good about themselves? How can educators get single parents to feel good about themselves? How can African American fathers play an active role in their child's education? These questions still baffle researchers, but considering the various obstacles Black boys face within the scope of education today, the Triple P program is a start in the right direction for mothers.

Chapter 5

Where Is My Father? (Songs from the Soul)

Proverb: Character is like smoke; it cannot be hidden.

❖

There are around 9 million Black families in the United States of America. In the Black family today, at least 63% of boys are raised by single mothers. Early research portrayed African American fathers as generally absent or uninvolved in their children's lives (*42*). In contrast, more recent findings on African American fathers paint a different picture. This research shows that African American fathers, across socioeconomic and residency statuses, are involved with and interested in their children, and can be nurturing and sensitive to their needs (*10*). Studies of resident fathers show that compared to White fathers, African Americans spend equivalent time in direct activities with their children and monitor their children more (*43*). Other, more nuanced findings show that fathers spend less time with their children during the week than during the weekend, and Black fathers have been found to spend more time on weekends relative to White fathers (*44*). The total amount of time spent with children and how it is divided across the days of the week may be less important for children's outcomes than the sensitivity and responsiveness of fathers during their time together (*45*). Unfortunately, one of the greatest challenges facing educators today is the lack of parental involvement by fathers.

During the time of slavery, Black boys usually didn't see Black men, especially fathers, in a positive manner. Their exposure consisted of Black men hanging from trees, serving the master, whipping other slaves, and dying by drastic means. Even today, 400 years after slavery, Black boys mostly see professional athletes or rappers as role models. I frequently ask educators questions related to this, like the following: How often do you see Black men shown in a negative manner on the news? How often does the news acknowledge the success of the Black father raising children? How often do they acknowledge Black men who are providers for their families? How often do you see positive Black men portrayed on television? Did you know almost 1 million Black fathers are raising children on their own?

Considering the state of Black boys in the school system, it's time to do something, fathers. I hope this chapter opens the eyes of fathers, especially fathers of Black boys. In my years as a professional school counselor, I've counseled thousands of young men, especially Black boys. One thing I have found is that around 90% of them are walking around emotionally traumatized from the lack of a father in their lives. In most of my sessions, I can see the yearning for their fathers. Even when the father is absent, they still yearn for a relationship. In my sessions with parents, especially fathers, I always ask, "What's the difference between a father and a dad?" The answer varies from person to person, of course, but based on what I've seen and the feedback I've received, I feel that fathers/dads seem to fall into the following song-related categories: First is the "Lean on Me" Fathers. They are very active fathers, and there's no question how they feel. Second is the "Smiling Face" fathers, who smile when they see you but take no action when it comes to parenting. Next is the "Back Stabber" fathers; they show up at school sometimes, and they talk a good game, but they never take any action. Sometimes they tell the truth; sometimes they don't. The child is confused, and so is the counselor. Last is the "Papa was a Rolling Stone" fathers. They are just trifling. There are not active in the lives of their children. They don't come to any school meetings, they're never around when you call, and they break promises. So I'm asking you this, fathers: which song are you singing? What tune do you need to change?

I recall presenting to 75 high schools kids from Homeland Security High in Baltimore City, Maryland. There were about 50 girls and 30 boys. These kids were coming from areas similar to the streets of Detroit, Chicago, and New York. The attendees were a diverse group of students, including honor roll students, average students, drop outs who had returned, and even those who skipped school and sold drugs. The principal wanted me to motivate them to stay in school, while keeping it real. I started off the session asking how many of them had heard of 50 Cent. They all raised their hand. I then asked, "Who can finish this title: 'Get ____ or Die ____.' They all knew it: "Get Rich or Die Trying." I used that as a springboard and then spoke to them on the theme "Get an Education or Get Locked Up."

During the workshop, I challenged the boys to be honest with themselves about what bothered them for most of their lives. We discussed manhood, womanhood, and how to open up and express your feelings. About three hours into the workshop, I played the song Dear Mama, by 2 Pac, which talks about his family. I asked the students in the room, "How did that relate to you?" For several moments, they just looked around in silence. Finally, one hand went up, followed by about eight more. The subsequent conversation was deep and insightful.

One young man stood up with tears in his eyes and said, "For seventeen years, I've always wanted my father in my life. I've never shared this with anyone, but I know if my father was around, I wouldn't be in this position today." He is one of the million boys, especially Black boys who suffer from the emotional incarceration of a father not being there.

Akbar (46) described the transition boys undergo as follows: "A male, a boy and a man are not the same thing. A male is a biological creature, a boy is a creature in transition, and a man is someone who has arrived to a purpose and a destiny." One of the goals of an elementary school counselor should be to help boys transition to manhood. Unfortunately, I believe that Black boys at the elementary level are in a state of emergency considering the fact that African American boys make up over 75% of the students placed in special education (5). Furthermore, sexism and racism play a significant role, based on the fact that 83% of teaching staffs are female and 92% are White (5). These statistics clearly show that there is an increasing amount of African American boys in special education and a small percentage of African American teachers. The chances of an African American boy going to school from kindergarten to the sixth grade without seeing a positive African American male is quite high. These statistics alone should send a message to men, especially fathers; the role of Black men at the elementary level is imperative, as these factors negatively affect the positive self-image that African American boys have of themselves in their early public school years.

Akbar (7) attempted to understand the chronic underperformance of disadvantaged minority students through examining the socio-cognitive dynamics of schooling and the academic environment, specifically the effects of negative group stereotypes. Akbar argued that the school environment is adverse to African American boys because of the negative stereotypes long before the achievement gap manifests itself. Akbar further argued that being continually immersed in an aversive environment can contribute to what he called dis-identification, the selective devaluing of academics and culture. As a result, one of the central points of African American male achievement has been dis-identification. Furthermore, African American boys associate education with a cool pose, which aligns education as White (15). Historically, when African American children have been given a Eurocentric and middle class viewpoint on education, they often feel devalued.

It's not by accident that 84% of African American boys aren't enrolled in gifted and talented classes (47).

Furthermore, African American boys are below a grade level in math (*4*). In contrast, White students outscore and remain ahead in all areas of education. These disproportionate results validate the stereotype that being White is smart, and that in the African American community, it is okay to be average. This belief is a result of the stereotypes that are portrayed in society and filtered right into the educational environment. Once these beliefs are filtered into the educational environment, evidence of these stereotypes becomes apparent. For example, according to Kunjufu (*5*), 65% of African American boys in kindergarten will not graduate from high school. In addition, every 46 seconds, an African American male student drops out of school. Furthermore, over 40% of African American males are illiterate in America.

One out of every three African American males is involved in the penal system, and they make up 30% of drug arrests, 55% of which lead to drug convictions. As a result, the school-to-prison pipeline is moving full speed ahead for African American boys, so much so that two out of every three African American males are projected to be in the penal system by the year 2020. For every 100,000 White males, 730 are incarcerated, a figure that only includes federal and state prisons; in contrast, for every 100,000 African American males, 3,250 are incarcerated in state and federal jails (*5*). According to Alexander (*48*), in Washington, DC, our nation's capital, it is estimated that three out of every four young Black men can expect to serve time in prison. Furthermore, one in three young African American men are currently under the control of the criminal justice system—in prison, in jail, on probation, or on parole—yet mass incarceration tends to be categorized as a criminal justice issue opposed to a racial justice or civil rights issue. As of 2008, there were approximately 2.3 million people in prisons and jails, and a staggering 5.1 million people under community correction supervision. Over half of the people locked up in prisons are Black males. Fathers, it's time to get involved and help change this bleak outlook for our sons.

As an elementary counselor, I would always challenge men in the community to get involved at the elementary level. There is an old saying that goes, "It takes a village to raise a child." If Black boys in the public school system are to grow into strong, educated, productive men, then a communal effort is essential. The effort should include fathers, professional Black men, Professional positive Black male athletes, Black males in the church, Black male college students, Black males in the high schools, and even retired Black males. A house is as strong as its foundation. With that said, Black fathers need to be present in the lives of their children, especially at the elementary level. There is no greater feeling than to see Black men playing active roles in the lives of Black boys. As a child, all I wanted was a father with a purpose and destiny. I wanted him to be the man who helped me with my school work, the man who would spank me when I was wrong, the man who took care of his responsibilities. Even though he wasn't perfect and lost focus of what was important, he was still my father. Seeing him when I did restored my faith. Because of the mistakes my father made, it took years for both of us to heal, but we did heal.

I'm challenging every father, especially African American fathers, to take this opportunity to forgive yourself, heal yourself, and love yourself. There is a child crying, yearning for you; please correct the wrong and go back with a purpose and destiny. I encourage every father reading this chapter, especially Black fathers, to pull up You Tube and type in "Be a Father to Your Child," by Ed G and the Bull Dogs. Watch the video and think about the words to the song. There is no theoretical paradigm that can convince a Black man to father his child, but I will leave you with this: Fathers, regardless of what you have done, there is a child waiting with open, forgiving arms. I was that child, and my father finally realized his purpose and destiny. It's your turn now.

Chapter 6

Post-Traumatic School Disorder Treatment

"The mind is like an umbrella; it functions when open." –Chibuzor Ogu

The psychological trauma inflicted on Black families during slavery is still present today. The impact is obvious based on the fact that there are Black boys not taking education seriously, failing school, dropping out of school and locked up. The questions asked by teachers, school counselors, mental health professionals, parents, pastors, and community workers are, "What is wrong with Black boys in public schools today? What can school counselors, teachers, and educators do to close the achievement gap?" Part of the answer lies in empowering Black boys through school counselor advocacy.

Traditional school counseling depends on counseling theory and approaches with little or no regard for cultural backgrounds. Emphasis is placed on individual student factors; little or no emphasis is placed on oppression or equality, and counseling usually takes place during the day. Traditional counseling uses labels to identify students, focuses on the status quo, and, finally, focuses on enrolling students in comfortable courses (*3*). During the latter part of the 20th century, counselors became increasingly aware of the unique needs of minority client populations. Thus, multicultural counseling competence became a critical component in the training of professional school counselors (*49*). Also, practitioners began to recognize that many students face significant environmental challenges and limitations to their well-being, and as a result, school counselor advocacy received a heightened focus in the counseling profession (*50*). Rooted in social action and activism, advocacy counseling emphasizes that counselors may play key roles in helping students identify oppressive policies and practices that may impede their success (*51*).

In 2004, the ASCA, recognizing the importance of advocacy in the counseling profession, began to include advocacy as a critical leadership component of comprehensive school counseling programs in its national model for school counseling. (*6*). Also emphasizing the role of advocacy, the Transforming School Counseling Initiative called upon school counselors to take an active role in helping minority and disadvantaged students receive needed support for achieving academic success (*52*). In addition, the Task Force on Advocacy Competencies of the American Counseling Association (ACA) developed a guiding set of principles to help counselors work from an advocacy perspective. The advocacy competencies are founded upon a social justice philosophy that acknowledges the impact of social, political, economic, and cultural factors on human development. These domains consist of client advocacy, community advocacy, and public advocacy. Furthermore, within each domain, counselors may act on behalf of their students or along with their students. A central aspect of this model involves client empowerment through self-advocacy. There are several definitions of self-advocacy; however, school counselors must align themselves by defining self-advocacy as the ability to assertively communicate or negotiate one's interests, desires, needs, and rights (53). In order for students to become self-advocates, they must first develop self-awareness and self-identity and become more knowledgeable about their specific needs. Thus, the primary objective of every professional school counselor should be to advocate. The school counselor as an advocate can ensure that all students have access to the information and experiences that will allow them to influence the society of the future (54).

In addition, the ASCA adopted a national model to address the needs of all students, especially African American boys. This approach focuses on using social justice counseling to meet the needs of African American boys. Social justice-based counseling represents a multifaceted approach to counseling in which practitioners strive to simultaneously promote human development and the common good through addressing challenges related to both individual and distributive justice through equity and equality (3). The primary goal of the social justice approach is to examine the sociocultural and environmental factors that influence students' behavior and performance. These factors include oppression, racism, classism, and sexism, which in some cases undermine the emotional and interpersonal well-being of students, thus potentially resulting in student underachievement and mental and emotional distress. The social justice approach to school counseling is centered on reducing the effects of oppression on students and improving equity and access to educational services. The social justice approach's major focus is on highlighting the strengths of students, emphasizing sociocultural and environmental factors that influence students' behavior and performance, and challenging oppression and oppressive practices. Emphasis is placed on equality and equity, which is implemented after school in some form of activity. During the activity, students are described by their strengths. The data provided from these activities focuses on changing existing policies and strategies for all students (*3*).

Currently, there are six key elements to school-based social justice counseling: counseling intervention and planning, consultation, connecting school families and communities, collecting and using data, challenging bias, and coordinating student services. Utilization of the social justice approach falls right in line with the ASCA national model, which focuses on accountability, the management system, the delivery system, and the foundation. The incorporation of the national model allows professional school counselors to apply culturally appropriate counseling interventions. One intervention, strength-based counseling, assesses and recognizes the inherent strength of students and builds on those strengths to create change (*55*). Empowerment-based counseling is a form of counselor advocacy where the counselor empowers the student to achieve goals, with the ultimate outcome of being able to help the student act independently in the future. Another intervention, Ethnic Identity Development counseling, requires the professional school counselor to make enhancing a student's ethnic and racial identity development a major priority when counseling. There are several other strategies for promoting self-advocacy among African American boys as well.

As leaders in the school system, professional school counselors are the catalyst for helping schools focus on the success of minority students (6). The self-advocacy competencies provide a framework for integrating self-advocacy skill development into a comprehensive school counseling program. This approach requires the teachers, parents, principals, and counselors to work collaboratively to ensure minority students receive ongoing encouragement to become self-advocates. There are a variety of strategies that may be used in comprehensive school counseling programs to address the need for self-advocacy among African American boys. According to Baggerly and Parker (56), by using culturally and developmentally appropriate interventions, self-advocacy awareness, knowledge, and skills may be fostered among students at all grade levels. In order to help African American boys develop awareness necessary for self-advocacy, school counselors may consider using self-reflective and experiential activities both individually and in groups. The following strategies are considered awareness-building strategies:

- At the elementary level, school counselors can use narrative activities and multicultural children's literature in small and large group guidance lessons to help students learn about their own cultural backgrounds and the diverse cultural heritage of others.
- At the elementary level, dramatic presentations and plays can help African American boys identify and respond to prejudice and oppression. School counselors can assist African American boys in increasing their self-advocacy knowledge through guidance presentations and activities designed to help students recognize prejudicial and oppressive practices. School counselors may encourage students to learn about how African American boys dealt with prejudice and oppression in the past by watching documentaries on slavery.
- At the elementary level, professional school counselors may form empowerment groups, which would allow African American boys to develop an action plan for promoting positive change in the school and community. African American boys may benefit from community and peer networking with other minority students in order to develop awareness of both individual and collective action in promoting minority student success.
- At all levels, writing and sharing cultural autobiographies may help students explore and value their cultural background.

- At all levels, encouraging students to participate in school-wide, cultural-centered programs and celebrations may help increase awareness and appreciation of diverse cultures.
- At all levels, school counselors may help promote self-advocacy knowledge by using bibliotherapy. Professional school counselors can also help African American boys promote self-advocacy by matching them with mentors via the church, community organizations, and volunteers.

These are excellent knowledge-building strategies that may help African American boys understand through dialogue the legacy of oppression in educational settings. In order to ensure systemic support for student self-advocacy, professional school counselors must provide training in the principles of social justice education for students, teachers, parents, and administrators. Overall, the objective should be to empower students through advocacy.

Chapter 7

Empowerment Program for Black Boys (Action, Attitude, Accountability)

"When your neighbor's horse falls into a pit, you should not rejoice at it, for your own child may fall into it too." –Yoruba

Empowerment programs have proved to provide benefits to youth and are expanding rapidly in schools (57). Empowerment programs allow educators to survey the student population to identify a need for themed counseling groups, create a mission and purpose for the themed group, create a creed or code of honor that represents the purpose for the themed group, recruit students who can benefit from the themed group, and collaborate with students to identify the goals and objectives that include activities and events for the themed group. Research has suggested that school mentoring programs may assist in the reduction of alcohol and drug use, teen parentage, gang membership, and peer violence. Studies have also reported that interpersonal skills and relationships have improved along with self-confidence, attitudes toward school, and academic achievement (57).

I first started implementing empowerment groups in 2000. One reason I started the groups was because of what I observed to be the lack of males, especially Black males, at the elementary level. I found the lack of Black males at this level shocking considering how important this primary age is in the development of Black boys. Since manhood has been reported historically as a complex task for Black males, it is imperative that their manhood is fostered at an early age by positive socializing agents and institutions. During this time period, Black boys start learning what it means to be a man. They start to develop images of manhood based on their exposure. It's during this time period when Black boys learn to be un-emotional. They will go into manhood never addressing the emotional trauma they experienced as a child. As a result, in manhood, they will exhibit certain behaviors no one can explain. When boys are taught to express their emotions, a major weight is taken off their shoulders. I've spoken to several grown men who have never discussed the trauma they experienced as a child. This helped me realize why it was important that young men are taught that it's okay to cry and express their emotions as children.

Another reason I started empowerment groups was because I observed that boys, especially African American boys, believed they were the only ones going through what they were going through. Once they were placed in a group where they all shared similar obstacles and challenges, they were able to learn from each other. Once boys are in a group environment where trust has been established, they will start opening up. Individual counseling and small-group counseling represent effective mediums for promoting healthy positive social behaviors among urban African American male adolescents. Such counseling approaches facilitate social/emotional well-being in maladaptive behaviors (58). All boys, especially Black boys, want to be part of a group.

My first initial group consisted of 12 Black males. I was supported to a degree by my principal, but she was mostly concerned with students being prepared for testing. What she and some administrators don't realize is that when boys are emotionally constipated, they will not perform to their ability. Finally, I transferred to a school where the principal supported my vision 100%, Ardmore Elementary School. In 2005, I started an intervention program called Men of Ardmore. The purpose of this intervention program was to promote leadership development, self-empowerment, self-efficacy, strength-based activities, and empowerment-based activities. The program consisted of 22 boys the first year, 35 the second year, and 55 the third year. The students were fifth- and sixth-graders. We adopted the following theme: "Discipline yourself and others won't have to." Our motto was "Action, Attitude, and Accountability." The boys were taught that when a car breaks down, you call Triple A, so when you have an emotional breakdown, you check your actions and attitude so you can be accountable (our own version of Triple A).

The program lasted three years, and the results were amazing. The president of the group was selected based on his potential strong leadership and past disciplinary referrals. The students were selected based on their academic achievement, past disciplinary referrals, potential leadership abilities, and teacher referrals. It was a 26-week program that followed each student from the beginning of the school year to the last day of school. A typical session started with good news and group affirmations. The good news reports allowed each member to share something positive from the past or current week. After each member shared his good news, we proceeded with reciting of virtues and activities. After the initial sessions, we spent around six sessions or more studying the historical aspect of slavery and Jim Crow. What I found was that once the boys were taught the persecution of slavery, they had a deep appreciation for success. The success of the program was measured based on the test scores of the Maryland standardized test. I also examined the progression of the SRI Reading Inventory. The SRI was given twice during the academic school year. Finally, I measured suspension rates, student referrals, and teacher feedback.

My first year was quite a challenge. I selected a president, Andre, who was emotionally constipated. However, I knew if I could get him to change, everyone would see it and respond accordingly. He was someone everybody looked up to, including the girls. When he was elected president, he couldn't believe it. He was really excited when he was given his shirt. After about 12 weeks in the program, he began to change, and the rest followed. Here was a young man emotionally constipated with no direction, but with a little empowerment, he changed the lives of so many. Then there was Justin. His father was in jail, and his mother was going crazy. He was on medication and angry all the time. After he had been in the program for two years, his mother was interviewed for an article about the program, and she stated:

> His grades have consistently gone up from C to B in most subject areas and some A's. His math scores have been very satisfactory, considering his problems in math. The benefits of this program have been enormous to my son academically, socially, and in terms of overall discipline. You have no idea how much I appreciate you. This program and Mrs. Allen really helped Justin turn the corner during a time when he could have easily went the other way. (59)

Justin told the reporter that he was "proud to be part of the organization." He also said, "I've changed a lot since I joined the program. I pay more attention to my lessons. I have learned to deal with my anger management issues and I get along with my friends" (59). Indeed, he had changed. We started a Little Men of Ardmore program for the little boys who were having difficulties in grades k-3. Several of the Men of Ardmore were assigned a little man to mentor. Justin always wanted to go help his little brother, who was in second grade. I can recall several occasions where Justin would rush to eat his lunch to help tutor his little brother. He was a young man who went from being constipated to becoming a man.

Next, there was John. He was hell on wheels. John was angry, frustrated, hard core, and disrespectful; he had a gang mindset and basically stayed in the principal's office. He was constantly suspended and had no remorse. His first year in the program was challenging. He had leadership abilities, but he just didn't know how to channel his energy. In the middle of the school year, John approached me requesting to be president the next year. I was shocked. Here was a Black boy who was struggling, but he wanted to be part of something. John saw how the current president had changed his behavior, and by whatever means necessary, he was going to be president. The following months, the leader in him started coming out. He was improving academically, he developed a very positive attitude, he stopped getting in trouble, and he took on more responsibilities in the group. He did have setbacks, but he was a different person and everyone could see it. Finally, he became president, and he was a tough leader.

When Tony Richards of 96.3 WHUR came to interview the Men of Ardmore for the *Steve Harvey Morning Show*, he requested to interview John. I recall that Tony asked John what his role was, and John responded, "I'm the president of MOA. My job is to oversee the other kids [in the program] so they can be a better example for the younger children [in Little Men of Ardmore] because a lot of the kids have problems and we're here to help them, so when they need an extra friend, we're here like brothers."

Even the teachers said positive things. Mr. Johnson stated, "There has been an improvement in attitude, their willingness to cooperate with peers, and they are excited to be with each other. Many of them are shifting directions for the better."

Mrs. Jennings stated, "It's very positive. The program helps the older boys culturally, academically, and socially. Clay gives them a sense of self-worth as Black boys."

One father stated, "We need programs like this school wide" (59).

Each year the program was in place, there were positive comments like these from parents, students, and teachers. I can also recall many special and eye-opening moments in our sessions. In one particular session, the boys were asked, "What would you like to do when you grow up?" Seventy percent said they wanted to be a football or basketball player. I wasn't surprised; that's the superficial reality to which they are exposed. I challenged the young men to get rid of that stinking thinking. They were required to learn one profession from each letter of the alphabet. We would sit in a circle and start with the first letter and proceed around to the end. I also challenged them to answer the question in a different way, as follows: "I want to be a productive citizen and give back to the community." We practiced that answer for 30 minutes.

Several months passed after this particular session, and we went on a field trip to Boarders bookstore in downtown Washington D.C. to see Jeanie Jones (WKYS 96.3) and one of the Washington Wizards. As we proceeded up the escalator, people turned to look at us. Here were seven young Black boys in their black t-shirts with MOA in bold metallic silver on the front and the school name, mascot, and "Action, Attitude, and

Accountability" on the back. Upon seeing us, a reporter became curious. She requested permission to speak to one of the boys, and she selected Andre. She asked the usual who, what, and where questions, and then she asked the million-dollar question: "What would you like to be when you grow up?"

Andre answered, "I want to become a productive citizen and give back to the community." She was speechless. The look on her face was amazing. Andre couldn't wait to tell the rest of the boys what happened that day. I was excited too.

These are just a few of the amazing stories and moments I remember. Of course there were setbacks, but overall the results of the program were amazing. Over 70% of the boys improved academically, and suspension rates went down almost 90%. I've included two figures on the following pages that illustrate the program data and results from 2005-2008.

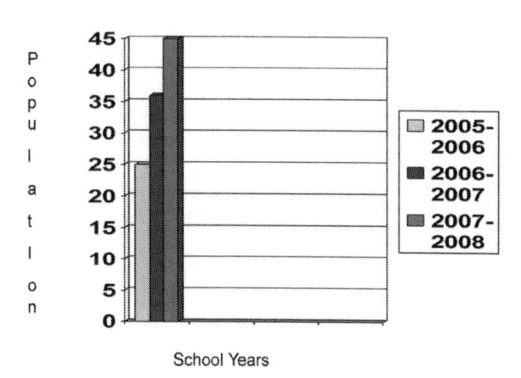

Figure 1. Men of Ardmore (MOA) students participating in the program.

Suspensions

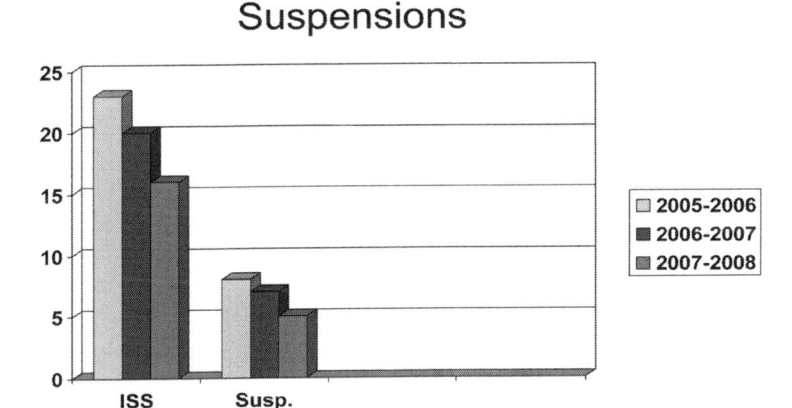

Figure 2. Program participant suspensions 2005-2008.

(Note: ISS = in-school suspension, Susp. = school suspension. In the 2007/2008 school year, three of the five suspensions were given to a new student to the school and organization.)

The results of my own empowerment program illustrate that professional school counselors must take a proactive approach in helping African American boys academically. In order for school counselors to help change inappropriate school behavior, they must understand the logic governing certain decisions of urban, African American male adolescents. Without this critical piece of information, many well-intentioned interventions will not succeed (60). By modeling the ASCA national standards and implementing a comprehensive strength- and empowerment-based counseling program, African American boys will become academically motivated to be successful. If professional school counselors are able to challenge old perceptions about the role of the school counselor and begin a paradigm shift that shows how professional school counselors are critical to the academic success of African American boys, then schools will be more open to helping African American boys in school.

Therefore, following is a guide to help counselors start an empowerment program. The challenges that confront African American boys in the school setting suggest a need for empowerment programs that focus on helping them socially and academically. Such initiatives should include self-empowerment, self-esteem, and self-development techniques. These initiatives could be implemented through classroom guidance, empowerment groups, group counseling, and individual counseling. Empowerment groups must start in elementary school and follow boys, especially Black boys, through high school. If implemented correctly, these initiatives should develop the positive attitudes, self-esteem, and self-identity of participants. As a result, there should be an improvement in academic achievement.

Setting Up an Empowerment Program

Student Selection: I recommend targeting the 5% of students who cause 95% of your problems. Include teacher, counselor, and parent recommendations. Also include honor roll students. Once the group is established, cut off membership. The boys will need time to build trust.

Group Attire: I recommend a black t-shirt with the group name on the front. If your school is Walker Elementary School, the shirt would read Men of Walker, with MOW underneath, or the other way around. Also, include something like "A Prestigious Organization Since 2011." I recommend they wear their shirts once or twice a month, and for special visitors. They must earn the right to wear their shirts.

Guest Speakers/Mentors: Seek Black male church leaders, alumni, fathers, radio personalities, fraternities, community organizations, custodial workers, middle school/high school staff, family members, co-workers, vice principals and principals from other schools, college students, and business owners.

Grade Levels: I recommend fifth and sixth grade for your program. If you have a Little Men program, I recommend k-4. If your school is k-5, adjust accordingly.

Meeting Times: I recommend meeting once a week for 30-45 minutes during their lunch and recess. This may change based on your school. In middle school, we met once a week for 1.5 hours after school.

Setting: The group should sit in a circle. The facilitator sits at the top end of the circle and is responsible for guiding the discussion. He must be part of the circle, as the circle symbolizes unity. I would not recommend that the facilitator stand in front of the group.

Facilitator: A Black or White male staff member with a deep understanding of African culture should facilitate. If possible, the boys should have access to this person throughout the day.

Sessions: The first three to six sessions should focus on setting rules, guidelines and group expectations; establishing the need for confidentiality; building rapport; and keeping it real.

The next six sessions should focus on slavery, the middle passage, and African culture. The students must learn from whence they came so they will know where they're going.

Parental Involvement: The parents must agree to meet with the facilitator. I think it is imperative that the parents are part of the process. Parents are more receptive when their child is going to be part of a group.

Topics: Recommendations include African history, Black history, slavery, racism, peer pressure, rap music, fatherhood, motherhood, entrepreneurship, fatherhood, family issues, violence in video games, character affirmations, violence, gangs, drugs, setting goals, and friendship. Several of the sessions may consist of watching various documentaries and movies about Black males and slavery.

Activities: Possibilities include father-son luncheon, mother-son luncheon, dances, field trips, community service trips, Dress-Up Day, Teacher Appreciation Day, and School Clean-Up Day. The activities may vary according to your school.

Chapter 8

Thinking Outside the Box (Social Media Counseling)

"Do not vacillate or you will be left in between doing something, having something and being nothing." –Ethiopia

One of the greatest challenges facing educators today is building rapport with Black boys. In several of my workshops, teachers have asked how to build rapport. My response to them has always been as follows: "Be genuine, show compassion, think outside the box, set high expectations, demand respect, infuse yourself in Black culture, take a field trip to their neighborhood, visit the church, listen and analyze rap and hip hop music, and show a little TLC (not tender loving care, but tough love and crazy)." One of the easiest ways to build rapport with Black boys is through rap, rhythm, rhyme, and music. During slavery, music was used to resist the spiritual brutality of slavery. In Africa, music had been a form of communication. Quite often, words were meaningless, but the music had tonal and rhythmic value. The slaves never lost the ability to communicate through music. Songs were used in every aspect of their lives. They sang for dancing and to ease the burden of work. They used music as a means of expressing their joy, sorrow, pain, and love for God. Music was so embedded in their spirit, they would use whatever objects were available to make music.

Four hundred years later, the rhythmic sounds of music are still present in the spirits of African Americans today. If you were to examine some of the successful schools in the United States, you would see that they are highly infused with Black culture or rhythmic forms of instruction. The Knowledge is Power Program (KIPP) in schools is a prime example of a rhythmic form of instruction. In my position as an elementary school counselor, I always had a love for music and rhythm. There was nothing more satisfying than to see children singing, clapping, and moving as they were engaged in the learning process. Because I was always looking for ways to build rapport with students, in 2000, I started an educational consulting practice called Rhyming to Respect, Creating Character in Children Incorporated. I realized then that if kids felt good about themselves, they could accomplish anything. From there, I started writing character education rhymes. As time progressed, I started infusing music into guidance lessons. As a result, I started using music as a counseling tool. Next, I started changing the lyrics of hip hop songs to reflect positive messages about respect. Now, I'm training teachers on how to infuse auditory music into instructional curriculum. This process not only builds rapport but engages kids in interactive learning.

In 2010, after several years as an elementary school counselor, I was presented with an opportunity for a middle school position. The school was 60% Black and

40% Hispanic. There I was moving from a mostly Black elementary school to a middle school with a large Hispanic population. I thought it was going to be a challenge. The timing was quite ironic because I had just returned from working with teachers in the Los Angeles School District. On the plane back, I was thinking, *I need to infuse myself with the Spanish culture.* I returned home, talked to God about it, and bam, the door was opened. I found myself at Charles Carroll Middle School in New Carrollton, Maryland.

I went in there on fire. The principal, Dr. Eric Wood, was just as excited as I was. I took that same passion I exhibited in elementary school and moved forward. I was in the hallways, classrooms, and cafeteria getting to know everyone. Every day, I would go in feeling empowered. Every morning at 6:00 a.m. was my time with God through listening to the *Steve Harvey Morning Show*, and I remember one morning about two months into my tenure, the topic of the day was how good God is and how with Him, anything is possible. I had started reading the life story of Associate Supreme Court Justice Sonia Sotomayor, and I began to want to do something to help Hispanic kids understand that anything was possible for them. I wrote a rap about the life of Justice Sotomayor using the beat from "Turn My Swag On," by Soulja Boy. I went to my principal with the idea of celebrating National Hispanic Heritage Month. I wanted to shoot a music video bringing African American and Hispanic kids together. He agreed, and several months later it was done. I told my principal and the kids that if Justice Sotomayor saw the video, she would visit our school. They thought I was crazy. I mailed the video to the Supreme Court in November 2009. Several months later, in January 2010, I was sitting at home checking my e-mail when I saw the e-mail that confirmed what I already knew, which was that with God, anything is possible. Basically, it said Justice Sotomayor wanted to visit my school. I couldn't wait to tell the kids.

You can imagine what it was like for the Hispanic children seeing her in real life. Justice Sotomayor shared words of inspiration that changed the lives of so many of my students. Several months later, the kids were still writing about her visit. Mrs. Wright, one of the language arts teachers, shared with me a letter that one of the Hispanic students wrote. The letter stated that after seeing the justice and hearing her tell them that hard work pays off, she knew she could accomplish anything. She went on to say she would strive to give her best. Her sentiments were shared by several other kids as well.

That visit was a highlight in my professional career. I felt like I was on top of the world because that was her first visit to any school. After her visit, much to my surprise, Justice Sotomayor sent me an autographed picture that said, "Mr. Clay, thank you for being such an extraordinary role model and leader." I would like to personally thank Associate Supreme Court Justice Sonia Sotomayor for inspiring my students and I. I would also like to thank Steve Harvey for his motivational minutes in the morning, which inspired me in the first place.

This inspiration led to the kids shooting a video for President Obama's health care bill. The students were also featured in the *Washington Post* and on Fox 5 News. I told my kids if President Barack Obama sees the video, he will visit the school. They think I'm crazy. Still, I sent the invitation, and I have faith that one day those kids and I will meet President Obama. This was a prime example of thinking outside the box. Here I was, an African American school counselor bringing African American and Hispanic kids together to celebrate National Hispanic Heritage Month. I'm sharing this story because when you have an idea, go for it. Don't allow anyone to deter you from implementing something that will bring about the social and academic development of children.

As I stated before, using rhythm, rhyme, and music is a good way to build rapport. The following are various character education rhymes and counseling lessons you can use to build rapport and enhance communication with Black boys. These lessons may be used in empowerment programs, individual sessions, group sessions, and classroom guidance. The objective is to use the words in the music to facilitate the communication between the adult and child.

Character Education Rhymes

Responsibility
(to the theme of "The Adams Family")

Da da da dum (snap snap)
Da da da dum (snap snap)
Da da da dum da da dum da da dum (snap snap)
I'm ready when I'm called on
My word is done I'm sure of
No talking out of turn of
Responsibility
My chores are done at home now
I can go outside and play, wow
My parents are impressed with my
Responsibility
Da da da dum (snap snap)
Da da da dum (snap snap)
Da da da (dum) Da da da (dum) Da da da dum (snap snap)
Da da da (dum) (I'm neat) Da da da dum (I'm sweet)
Da da da dum Da da da dum Da da da dum (work's complete)
I'm listening and I'm learning
Respecting other's feelings
I'm handling my business
Responsibility

Good Attitude

(to the tune of "Mary Had a Little Lamb")

Mark had a good attitude
Good attitude
Good attitude
Mark had a good attitude
and his behavior showed
Everywhere that Mark went
Mark went
Mark went
Everywhere that Mark went, his attitude was sure to show
It followed him to class one day
Class one day
Class one day
It followed him to class one day
Which was very cool
Now the teacher has happy days
Happy days
Happy days
Now the teacher has happy days
Which made her day smooth
Your attitude determines your altitude

Concentration

(to the theme of "The Flintstones")

Concentration, meet Concentration
It's part of learning
From the town of Concentration
You need it when listening
Pay attention, look and listen is a street
Practice it and good grades you will keep
When practicing Concentration, you will know it's school time, a dabba school time, we'll have a nice old time.

Think About It

(to the tune of "If You're Happy and You Know It")

When you make a mistake, think about it
When you don't cooperate, think about it
When you're talking in class and you're not on task
you really need to think about it
When you're not paying attention, think about it
When you don't want to listen, think about it
When your grades are really bad and you start feeling sad
correct what is wrong, think about it
When you don't follow rules, think about it
You're here to learn in school, think about it
When you're doing something wrong, correct what is wrong
and listen to the song, think about it
I'm ready to learn, think about it
Good grades I'm going to earn, think about it
When my mind is on task, I know I will pass
my family will be glad, think about it
Always try your best in school, think about it
Learning can be cool, think about it
I want to apologize for all my mistakes in the past
but now I'm on task, think about it!

Honesty

(to the theme of "The Beverly Hillbillies")

Here's a story about a boy named Ned
A poor fourth grader things were never what he said
Then one day he was shooting out a lie
and up came his teacher saying "What's your alibi?"
"Didn't do it," he said. "Wasn't me!"
He failed the test on honesty
Well the next thing you know, ol' Ned thinks he's cool
Friend folk say, "But you're a lying fool!
Telling the truth is the place you want to be!"
So he cleaned up his act and turned to honesty
Old Ned found some new friends the day he changed his ways
He doesn't have to sneak around plotting out his days
He learned to tell the truth
and guess what people started to say,
"You can believe everything that Ned has to say!"
The moral of the story, which holds true,
telling a lie will stick to you like glue
So take my advice and listen to me
so we can tell the truth in elementary

Song-Based Lessons

"I Believe I Can Fly"

Goal: To help students develop self-esteem.
Objective: To help students develop a positive self-image.
Set the Stage: Define and discuss the two types of self-esteem (High/Low).
Degree of Learning: Have students write down/discuss what they want to be when they grow up.
Understanding of Learning: Explain that you are going to play a song. Ask students to close their eyes and pay attention. Play the song and then ask the following:

- What is the name of song?
- What type of self-esteem does he have and why?
- He believes he can what?
- What did he say starts with you?
- He stated he was on the verge of what?
- The songs says he knows the true meaning of what?
- How does the song relate to you?

Review Learning: Ask the following:

- Why was he successful in the song?
- What did you learn from this song?

Closure: Ask the following:

- What are the two types of self-esteem, and how do you build self-esteem?

- Who is the person that can stop you?
- What is the hook?

Activity: Go to You Tube and type in "I Believe I Can Fly," by R. Kelly. Watch, analyze, and discuss during or after the session.

"Runaway Love"

Goal: To help students deal with the feelings of emotional and physical abuse.
Objective: To help students open up and discuss their feelings.
Set the Stage: Discuss the various types of abuse.
Degree of Learning: Ask students to write down/say the name of someone who has hurt them.
Understanding of Learning: Explain that you are going to play a song. Ask students to close their eyes and pay attention. Play the song and then ask the following:

- Hold old is Lisa?
- What happened to her daddy and her mother?
- Who didn't believe her?
- Why did she say, "Ouch"?
- How did you feel after hearing this song?
- How old is Nicole?
- What did her stepfather do to her?
- Who was her friend?
- What happened to her friend?
- Why did Nicole run away?
- What could have Nicole done?
- How old was Erica?
- What did she do to get rid of the pain?
- Why did she go to the doctor?
- How did she solve her problem?
- How do you see your life in this song?

Review of Learning: Ask the following:

- How do you feel after hearing this song?
- What did you learn from this song?
- Name something positive from the song.

Closure: Discuss the importance of sharing feelings and the importance of seeking help until someone listens. Ask, "What is the hook?"

Activity: Go to You Tube and type in "Runaway Love," by Ludacris/Mary J. Blige. Watch, analyze, and discuss during or after the session.

"Locked Up"

Goal: To keep students out of prison.
Objective: To discuss prison life.
Set the Stage: Ask students to tell you how many Black males are in prison. Discuss.
Degree of Learning: Ask the participants to name Black males they know who are currently locked up. How do they feel about them and why?
Understanding of Learning: Explain that you are going to play a song. Ask students to close their eyes and pay attention. Play the song and then ask the following:

- What is the name of the song?
- Why is he stressed?
- What happened to his car?
- What color are the walls?
- What color are the clothes?
- What's wrong with the phone?
- How does the food taste?
- Who was dressed undercover?
- Who forget about him?
- What did Akon mean when he said "trying to figure out why I do what I do"?
- What's not getting any closer? What does that mean?
- Why was visitation hard to come by?
- He can't wait to do what?

Review of Learning: Ask the following:

- How did you feel after hearing this song?
- What was Akon really saying?

Closure: Ask the following:
- What did you learn from this song?
- Why did he write this song?

Activity: Go to You Tube and type in "Locked Up," by Akon. Watch, analyze, and discuss during or after the session.

"Mockingbird"

Goal: To help students discuss family issues.
Objective: To help students understand their feelings.
Set the Stage: Define family. Discuss why family is important.
Degree of Learning: Ask students to discuss or write down the names of family members important in their lives. Discuss why they are important. Discuss why they hurt them. Discuss how to forgive people in the family.
Understanding of Learning: Explain that you are going to play a song. Ask students to close their eyes and pay attention. Play the song and then ask the following:

- What is the name of the song?
- Where is her mother?
- Where is her father?
- What did her father want to give her?
- Why were they confused?
- Why did she cry at Christmas?
- What happened to the house she lived in?
- What habit did her mom develop?
- Why did her mom save money?
- What was Eminem reminiscing about?
- How do you see yourself in the song?

Review of Learning: Ask the following:

- How did you feel after hearing the song?
- What did you learn from this song?
- Name something positive from the song.

Closure: Discuss the importance of sharing feelings. Discuss the importance of forgiveness. Ask, "What is the hook?"

Activity: Go to You Tube and type in "Mockingbird," by Eminem. Watch, analyze, and discuss during or after the session.

"Dear Mama"

Goal: To develop an appreciation for parents.
Objective: To foster a better relationship with mothers.
Set the Stage: Discuss the importance of mothers in the lives of boys.
Degree of Learning: Ask students to write down 10 things they like about their mother or motherly figures. Discuss.
Understanding of Learning: Explain that you are going to play a song. Ask students to close their eyes and pay attention. Play the song and then ask the following:

- What is the name of the song?
- What happened at the age of 17?
- What happened at school?
- Who did they blame?
- What thoughts did 2Pac have in elementary school?
- His mother was a what?
- What did 2Pac finally understand?
- Why was he angry at his father?
- Who could he depend on?
- Why did he hang around thugs?
- Why did 2Pac appreciate his mother?

Review of Learning: Ask the following:

- How did 2Pac feel about his mother?
- How did you feel listening to this song?
- How do you relate to this song?
- Did 2Pac's mothers love him? Why?

Closure: Ask the following:

- What did you learn from this song?
- What are you going to tell the motherly figure in your life?

Activity: Go to You Tube and type in "Dear Mama," by 2Pac. Watch and analyze during or after the session.

"Keep Your Head Up"

Goal: To help boys gain more respect for mothers.
Objective: To help boys appreciate the women in their life.
Set the Stage: Discuss why women are important in the lives of boys.
Degree of Learning: Have students discuss something a woman has done to help them.
Understanding of Learning: Explain that you are going to play a song. Ask students to close their eyes and pay attention. Play the song and then ask the following:

- What is the name of the song?
- What did 2Pac say young brothers do?
- What did Marvin Gaye say?
- What did his mother do for him?
- What happened to his friends?
- What happened to his boy's family?
- Where was his daddy?
- What did he mean when he said "conquer this insanity"?
- What did 2Pac mean when he said his mother was dying inside but was fearless?
- How do you see yourself in the song?

Review of Learning: Ask the following:

- How did you feel after hearing this song?
- What did you learn from this song?
- Name something positive from the song.

Closure: Ask the following:
- What message was 2Pac sending in this song?
- How did 2Pac feel about women?

Activity: Go to You Tube and type in "Gotta Keep Your Head Up," by 2Pac. Watch and analyze during or after the session.

The counselor should use self-reflection when conducting the music sessions. This will help build a comfort level between the student and counselor. Below is a list of songs that may be used to facilitate conversation between parents and children. They may also be used by mental health professionals, school counselors, and adults working with youth in any capacity. Furthermore, they can be used by classroom teachers for writing purposes, homework assignments, and class discussions.

Title	Artist	Topic
Why Is That	KRS-One	Black History
You Must Learn	KRS-One	Black History
My Philosophy	Boogie Down Productions	Black History
Stop Violence	KRS-One	Black History
*Dead Gone	T.I.	Making Positive Choices
*Better Day	T.I.	Setting Goals
*The Light	Common	Respect for Love/Women
The 6th Sense	Common	Greed/Streets/Society
Children's Story	Slick Rick	Making Positive Choices

*Message	Grandmaster Flash	Drugs, Education, Prison, Streets, Survival
Wake Up	Brand Nubians	Black Culture
Slow Down	Brand Nubians	Making Positive Choices
Changes	2Pac	Making Positive Choices
*Brenda Got a Baby	2Pac	Teenage Pregnancy
*Go See the Doctor	Kool Moe Dee	Sex
Letter 2 My Unborn Child	2Pac	Survival
Hold On Be Strong	2Pac	Street Love
So Many Tears	2Pac	Pain
*Got My Mind Made Up	2Pac	Hard Core Life
I Ain't Mad at Cha	2Pac	Forgiveness
Cradle to Grave	2Pac	Birth, Prison, Death
*White Man's World	2Pac	Racism
*Me Against the World	2Pac	Conscience
*Only God Can Judge Me	2Pac	Conscience
Lord Knows	2Pac	Seeking God
Good Die Young	2Pac	Love

Lord Show Me a Sign	D.M.X.	Survival
Be a Father to Your Child	Ed. G	Fatherhood
I Can	N.A.S.	Self-Esteem
Fabulous	Jaheim	Self-Esteem
Hopeful	Twista	Hope
Superstar	Lupe Fiasco	Self-Esteem
*My Mind Playing Tricks on Me	Geto Boys	Reality
Self Destruction	KRS-One	The Reality for America
Friends	Whodini	Friends
Timex Social Club	Rumors	Rumors
Hate on Me	Jill Scott	Envy, Jealousy

*Please make sure the lyrics are age appropriate.

I selected several songs by 2Pac because his lyrics represent the true essence of life for most Black boys. The lyrics for the songs listed above may be found by typing the title and name in an Internet search box. The videos may be heard or seen by following the You Tube instructions in the lessons. In addition, for the real 2Pac, not the media depiction, go to You Tube and type in "Tupac Uncensored and Uncut Prison Video" and watch and listen. Furthermore, type in "1994 2Pac Interview with Ed Gordon Part 1, 2, 3" and watch and listen. The videos are excellent for classroom guidance, group counseling, individual counseling, parents, and communicating with youth.

Chapter 9

Conclusion

In conclusion, based on my interactions with students, parents, teachers, other counselors, and administrators, as well as the findings from my empowerment program, I propose the following recommendations:

- The role of professional school counselors should match the standards set by the ASCA national model.
- School systems nationally should adopt counseling policies that will enhance the academic achievement of Black boys.
- Professional school counselors should continue to participate in professional development trainings.
- Counseling supervisors should take an active role in supporting professional school counselors.
- Administrators should allow counselors to do their jobs.
- Professional school counselors should collaborate with other counselors about techniques that will help boys, especially Black boys.
- School counselors should implement strength-based and empowerment techniques when counseling boys, especially Black boys.

- School counselors must include more programs to get Black men involved in the school setting.
- School counselors should place an emphasis on African culture when counseling Black boys.

Certainly, one of the greatest challenges of school counselors today is helping African American boys academically and socially. Over the past several years, I've come to the conclusion that counselors must take a proactive approach in helping African American boys socially and academically. By modeling the ASCA national standards and implementing a comprehensive empowerment counseling program, African American boys will become academically motivated to be successful. If professional school counselors are able to challenge old perceptions about the role of the school counselor and begin a paradigm shift that shows how school counselors are critical to the academic success of African American boys, then schools will be more open to helping African Americans socially and academically. This paradigm shift will require professional school counselors to become advocates for African American boys. This shift must include parents, teachers, mental health counselors, mentors, educators, principals, and, most importantly, the professional school counselor. Once the shift is implemented correctly, we should see a difference in the academic and social abilities of African American boys.

Appendix A

The Alphabet of Life

❖

A. Action Attitude Accountability: You are responsible for your actions.
B. Ballers Ball: Always get it done.
C. Constructive Criticism Controls Crisis: Positive criticism is okay.
D. Develop Divine Discipline: Practice discipline at all times.
E. Exemplify Excellence: Give 110% at all times.
F. Forget Foolish Friends: Don't hang with negative people.
G. Gracious Goodness: Seek to help people.
H. Humble Himself: Always stay humble. It's not about you.
I. Inner Identity: Know thyself, know your history.
J. Journey Jovial: Seek to stay positive.
K. Kemetic Knowledge: Know your African heritage.
L. Love Language: Practice positive language.
M. Manners Make Millions: Don't get it twisted. Respect pays.
N. Never Nonsense: Think before you act.
O. Ordained Organization: Seek guidance and direction if confused.

P. Prepare Plan Perform Purpose: Have a plan when seeking to complete goals.
Q. Quality Quietism: It's better to listen than to speak.
R. Respect Returns Rapidly: People will remember you because our youth lack respect.
S. Serve Seriously: Give back to the community.
T. Transition Transformation: You can always change for the better.
U. Underachievement Ultimately Underserves: There is no excuse for underachievement.
V. Vibrant Vibes: Exemplify positive vibes at all times.
W. Wonderfully Woven: You were woven from queens and kings.
X. Xanthate: You are the salt of the earth.
Y. Yearn Yearly: Strive to better yourself and your community.
Z. Zealous Zest: Do you, but make sure it's positive.

These words may be used to reinforce character. They should be taught repetitiously.

Appendix B

Parenting Strategies

- Do not spoil your children or make excuses because the father is not present.
- You cannot be friends with your child.
- Raise your son to be emotional.
- Do not introduce your child to various men.
- Teach your child to clean, cook, and maintain the house.
- Spend quality time outside of school with your child.
- Spare the rod, spoil the child.
- Watch movies and documentaries on slavery.
- Watch the movie *Malcolm X* and discuss it.
- Never put your child's father down in front of him.
- Never argue with his father in front of him.
- Spend quality time at school with your child.
- Never become overprotective.
- Your child's pants should never hang down.
- Seek a positive male mentor for your son.
- Don't seek men who are models. Seek men who are role models.
- Study Egyptian (African) culture with your son.
- How you treat your son is how he will treat other women.

Appendix C

Parent Involvement Strategies for Teachers and Administrators

- Host a back-to-school night after Christmas break (the remix). This is in addition to back to school night in the fall. Use this time to discuss the state mandated test and to motivate the parents, students, and school community.
- Organize a Madden video game tournament between fathers: This will draw fathers out. A parent- teacher conference can be held before to discuss rules of the competition and academic concerns.
- Set a day once a month for parents to visit the school. Give it a creative name, like Magnificent Monday, Teacher Tuesday, Wonderful Wednesday, Thirsty Thursday, or Fun Friday. Serve food if possible.
- Set up conferences outside regular hours. For example, during parent-teacher conference day, set up conferences outside of usual hours. Allow the teachers to come in late if they agree to stay until 7 p.m. This will allow parents who can't get off work to attend.

- Use game shows to present information to parents. Parents love competition. For example, play Family Feud to discuss test-taking strategies.
- Establish a Reading Restaurant. Decorate the area like a restaurant and select books to read. Each section of the area should be named after a restaurant. The teachers serve the parents books and snacks. The administration serves as managers. You may add more ideas.
- Host a "Books, Bears, and Blankets" night. This is a reading night activity. The students and parents are allowed to wear pajamas and slippers. Each grade level reports to a designated area and selects a book to read. Students may be selected to read certain parts of each book. Snacks should be served, if possible. You may add more ideas.
- Host a Father-Son Luncheon and/or a Mother-Son Luncheon (all-day event).
- Host a Field Day (add-day event).
- Host Grandparent's Day (all-day event).
- Host Career Day (every school should have a Career Day).

Appendix D
Empowerment Resources

Videos and Movies
- *Roots*
- *Slavery: The Making of America* (Morgan Freeman)
- *The Middle Passage*
- *A War for Your Soul*
- **African Origins of Math and Civilization* (Chike Akua, teachertransformation.org)
- *Men II Boys* (Jakes Morton)
- *Malcolm X* (Spike Lee)
- *2Pac: The Resurrection*
- *Saving God* (Vin Rhames)

Books
- *Keeping Black Boys Out of Special Education*
- *Reducing the Black Male Dropout Rate*
- *An African Centered Response to Ruby Payne's Poverty Theory*
- *200+ Educational Strategies to Teach Children of Color*
- *Hip Hop Street Curriculum*
- *Understanding Black Male Learning Styles* (Dr. Jawanza Kunjufu)
- *Words of Power (Chike Akua)
- *Egypt on the Potomac: Nile Valley Contribution to Civilization* (Anthony Browder)

- *__Motivating Black Males to Achieve in School & In Life__* (Baruti Kafele)
- *Through Ebony Eyes: What Teachers Need to Know but Are Afraid to Ask About African American Students*
- *Other People's Children: Cultural Conflict in the Classroom* (Lisa Delpit)
- *We Can't Teach What We Don't Know* (Gary Howard)
- *Super Teaching* (Eric Jensen)
- **A Rose that Grew from the Concrete* (2Pac Shakur)
- *Black Children* (Janice Hale)
- *Learning While Black* (Janice Hale)
- *Marva Collins Way* (Marva Collins)
- *Ordinary Children/Extraordinary Teachers* (Marva Collins)
- *I Choose to Stay* (Salome Thomas-El)
- *From Rage to Hope: Strategies for Reclaiming Black and Hispanic Students* (C. Kuykendall)
- *African-Centered Interdisciplinary Multi-Level Hands-On Science* (Bernida Thompson)
- *Positive Afrikan Images for Children* (Social Studies Curriculum)
- *How to Teach Math to Black Students* (Shahid Muhammad) *__Least We Forget__* (Velma Maia Thomas)

Other

- *__Edlyrics.Com Hip Hop Educational Literacy Program__, 1-877-EDLYRICS

*Highly Recommended

Appendix E

A Teacher Counselor

❖

A teacher is a counselor and a counselor is a teacher. However, As the World Turns and we realize we have One Life to Live, then we will know a counselor is a teacher and a teacher is a counselor.

A teacher is the Guiding Light to a child who is Home Alone. Even though the money is low, your Passion for teaching is Bold and Beautiful. Some days the children will act like they're Young and Restless. Therefore, you start to think they belong in Another World. Then you realize they're All My Children.

A teacher is a counselor and a counselor is a teacher, and because of you, they will not end up in General Hospital. Their education will allow them to cruise into the Love Boat to Fantasy Island, where they will have a Good Time.

A teacher is a counselor and a counselor is a teacher, and because of you, they will have Happy Days. Thirty years from now, as they grow older and have children, they will tell them they were Touched By An Angel. That's why a teacher is a counselor and a counselor is a teacher.

Appendix F
Don't Let Go

◆⋮⋮◆

Please, Mom, don't let go. My life has really been a mess. I act the way I do because since my birth, my life has been a wreck. The beatings and mistreating by family members on crack. The nightly sounds of gun fire. I made it this far, no turning back. Please help, but whatever you do, don't let go. I want to live, but life's problems have really been tough. Family always tripping, Dad always sipping. He never had time for my mind; the only thing important to him was drinking all the time. I've seen it all growing up drugs, sex, physical abuse, emotional misuse and when I look at my life, tears fall down my eyes. My tears show the pain of a life lived in vain; however, those tears are temporary, your love is eternal. See, I was born with a smile. A smile that has traveled the ups and downs, smiles and frowns, of a million miles. Even though I'm only nine, I'm contemplating suicide, divorce is on the rise, drugs taking over our minds, young men pulling time, guns in school, students dropping out, that's not cool. I ask myself what is there left to do? Then I realize you're the apple of my eye. Thanks for helping me through.

Dr. William "Flip" Clay

About the Author

Dr. William "Flip" Clay is the CEO of Rhyming to Respect, LLC. He is a dynamic, energetic, creative, and nationally acclaimed consultant, writer, and speaker who has been featured on several radio stations, including the *Steve Harvey Morning Show* with Mr. Tony Richards. Dr. Clay was also featured in the education section of the *Washington Post*, and WTTG/WDCA Fox 5 News in Washington, DC, recognized Dr. Clay for bringing African American and Latino students together.

In 2010, United States Supreme Court Justice Sonia Sotomayor recognized Dr. Clay as an extraordinary role model and leader. Dr. Clay is the founder and creator of Men of Ardmore (MOA), a successful data-driven elementary-based male empowerment program, as well as Afro-Lino, a male empowerment program bridging the academic and social gaps between African American and Latino males. He is also a member of several professional organizations that include the National Alliance of Black School Educators, the Association of Supervision and Curriculum Development, and Phi Beta Sigma Fraternity Inc.

A graduate of Charleston Job Corps, Dr. Clay holds an undergraduate degree from West Virginia State College and a graduate degree from Virginia State University.

Dr. Clay recently completed his doctoral degree from Argosy University in Washington DC.

Dr. Clay is available for professional development, counselor workshops, student workshops, parent workshops, conferences, churches, colleges, youth organizations, etc. For more information, please visit http://www.RhymingtoRespect.com, send an e-mail to flip@rhymingtorespect.com, or call 1-877-787-6570. You can also connect with Dr. Clay through the following: Twitter as Dr_Flip, Facebook as Dr. William Clay, and Linkedin as Dr. William "Flip" Clay.

References

1. Lambie, G. W., & Williamson, L. L. (2004). The challenge to change from the guidance to professional school counseling: A historical proposition. *Professional School Counseling, 8,* 124-132.
2. Niebuhr, K. E., Niebuhr, R. E., & Cleveland, W. (1999). Principal and counselor collaboration. *Education, 199,* 674-678.
3. Holcomb-McCoy, C. (2007). *School counseling to close the achievement gap.* Thousand Oaks, CA: Corwin Press.
4. Kunjufu, J. (2005). *Keeping black boys out of special education.* Chicago, IL: African American Images.
5. Kunjufu, J. (2001). *State of emergency: We must save African American males.* Chicago, IL: African American Images.
6. American School Counselor Association. (2004). American School Counselor Association national model: Executive summary. *Professional School Counseling, 6*(3), 165-168.
7. Akbar, N. (2007). *Know thyself.* Tallahassee, FL: Mind Productions & Associates.
8. American Psychiatric Association. (2000). *Diagnostic and statistical manual of mental disorders* (revised 4th ed.). Washington, DC: Author.
9. Hooks, B. (1994). *Teaching transgress: Education as the practice of freedom.* New York, NY: Rutledge.

10. Ahmeduzzaman, M., & Roopnarine, J. L. (1992). Sociodemographic factors, functioning style, social support and fathers' involvement with preschoolers in African American families. *Journal of Marriage & Family, 54,* 699-707.
11. Hernstein, R., & Murray, A. L. (1994). The bell curve: Intelligence and class structure in America Life. New York, NY: Free Press.
12. Litwack, L. F. (2009). "Fight the power!" The legacy of the civil rights movement. *Journal of Southern History, 75,* 1-23.
13. Gay, G. (2000). Culturally responsive teaching theory research & practice. Amsterdam, NY: Teacher College Press.
14. Ogbu, J. U. (2003). Black students in an affluent suburb: A story of academic disengagement. Mahwah, NJ: Lawrence Erlbaum Associates.
15. Majors, R. (2001). Educating our children: New directions and radical approaches. New York, NY: Routledge Falmer.
16. DuBois, W. E. B. (1996). *The soul of Black folk.* New York, NY: Penguin Classics. (Original work published 1903)
17. Tatum, A. (2005). *Teaching reading to Black males: Closing the achievement gap.* Portland, ME: Stenhouse.
18. Bandura, A. (1997). *Social learning theory.* Englewood Cliffs, NJ: Prentice-Hall.
19. Cokley, K. (2003). What do we know about the academic motivation of African American college students? Challenging the "anti-intellectual myth." *Harvard Educational Review, 73,* 524-558.

References

20. Oyserman, D., Gant, L., & Ager, J. (1995). A socially contextualized model of African American identity: Possible selves and school persistence. *Journal of Personality and Social Psychology, 69*, 1216-1232.
21. Ford, D. Y., & Harris, J. J. (1997). A study of the racial identity and achievement of Black males and females. *Roper Review, 20*, 105-110.
22. Thomas, V. M. (1997). *Lest we forget: The passage from Africa to slavery and emancipation.* New York, NY: Crown.
23. Stamp, K. (1984). *The peculiar institution.* New York, NY: Random House.
24. Lester, J. (1998). *To be a slave.* New York, NY: Penguin Group.
25. Marrow, A. (2003). *Breaking the curse of Willie Lynch: The science of slavery psychology.* Florissant, MO: Rising Sun Publications.
26. Comer, P., & Poussaint, A. F. (1992). *Raising black children: Two leading psychiatrists confront the educational, social and emotional problems facing Black children.* New York, NY: The Penguin Group.
27. Fan, X. (2001). Parental involvement and students' academic achievement: A growth modeling analysis. *Journal of Experimental Education, 70*, 27-61.
28. Mandara, J., & Murray, C. B. (2002). Development of an empirical typology of African American family functioning. *Journal of Family Psychology, 16*, 318-337.
29. Collins, W. A., Maccoby, E. E., Steinberg, L., Heterington, E. M., & Borstein, M. H. (2000). Contemporary research on parenting: The case for nature and nurture. *American Psychologist, 55*, 218-232.

30. Rasheed, J. M., & Rasheed, M. N. (1999). Social work practice with African American men: The invisible presence. Thousand Oaks, CA: Sage.
31. Kumpfer, K. L., & Alvardo, R. (2003). Family-strengthening approaches for the prevention of youth problem behaviors. *American Psychologist, 58,* 457-465.
32. Ruggles, S. (1994). The origins of African American family structure. *American Sociological Review, 59,* 136-151.
33. Mandara, J. (2006). The impact of family functioning on African American males' academic achievement: A review and clarification of the empirical literature. *Teacher College, 108*(2), 206-233.
34. Battle, J., & Scott, B. (2000). Mother-only versus father-only households: Educational outcomes for African American males. *Journal of African American Men, 5*(2), 93-116.
35. Ferley, J. E. (2000). *Majority-minority relations.* Upper Saddle River, NJ: Prentice Hall.
36. Brewer, R. M. (1995). Gender, poverty, culture, and economy: Theorizing female-led families. In B. J. Dickerson (Ed.), *African American single mothers: Understanding their lives and families* (pp. 164-178). Thousand Oaks, CA: Sage.
37. Battle, J. (1999). How the boyz really made it out of the hood: Educational outcomes for African American boys in father only versus mother only households. *Race, Gender, & Class, 6*(2), 130-146.
38. Kunjufu, J. (1988). *To be popular or smart: The black peer group.* Chicago, IL: African American Images.

References

39. Norment, L. (2011 August). How parents influence how their sons and daughters view their dates, spouses and the world—Parenting. *Ebony, 58*(8). Retrieved from http://findarticles.com/p/articles/mi_m1077/is_8_58/ai_102025499/
40. McCollum, W. (2004). *Strength of a Black man: Destined for self-empowerment.* Washington, DC: The Empty Canoe.
41. Sanders, M. (2008). Triple P-Positive Parenting Program as a public health approach to strengthening parenting. *Journal of Family Psychology, 22*(3), 506-517.
42. McAdoo, J. L. (1993). The roles of African American fathers: An ecological perspective. *Families in Society, 74*(1), 28-35.
43. Hofferth, S. M. (2003). Race/ethnic differences in father involvement in two-parent families: Culture, context or economy? *Journal of Family Issues, 24*, 246-268.
44. Yeung, W. J., Sandberg, J., Davis-Kean, P. E., & Hofferth, S. L. (2001). Children's time with fathers in intact families. *Journal of Marriage & Family, 63*, 136-154.
45. Tamis-LeMonda, C. S., Rodriquez, V., Ahuja, P., Shannon, J. D., & Hannibal, B. (2002). Caregiver child affect, responsiveness, and engagement scale (C-CARES). Unpublished manuscript.
46. Akbar, N (2006). *Vision for black men.* Tallahassee, FL: Mind Production & Associates.
47. Wynn, M. (2007). Teaching, parenting, and mentoring successful black males. Marietta, GA: Rising Sun.

48. Alexander, M. (2010). *The new Jim Crow: Mass incarceration in the age of colorblindness.* New York, NY: The New Press.
49. Vera, E. M., & Speight, S. L. (2003). Multicultural competence, social justice, and counseling psychology: Expanding our roles. *The Counseling Psychologist, 31,* 253-272.
50. Ivey, A. E., & Collins, N. M. (2003). Social justice: A long term challenge for counseling psychology. *The Counseling Psychologist, 31,* 290-298.
51. Toporek, R. L., & Liu, W. M. (2001). Advocacy in counseling: Addressing issues of race, class and gender oppression. In D. B. Pope-Davis & H. L. K. Coleman (Eds.), *The intersection of race, class, and gender in counseling psychology* (pp. 385-416). Thousand Oaks, CA: Sage.
52. Education Trust. (2003). *Achievement in America.* Retrieved from http://www2.edtrust.org
53. Pearl, C. (2004). Laying the foundation for self-advocacy. *Teaching Exceptional Children, 36,* 44-49.
54. Stone, C., & Turba, R. (1999). School counselors using technology for advocacy. *Journal of Technology in Counseling, 30,* 63-77.
55. Ungar, M. (2006). *Strengths-based counseling with at-risk youth.* Thousand Oaks, CA: Corwin Press.
56. Baggerly, J., & Parker, M. (2005). Child centered group play therapy with African American boys at the elementary school level. *Journal of Counseling & Development, 83,* 387-396.
57. Dappen, L., & Iserhagen, J. C. (2006). Urban and nonurban schools: Examination of a statewide

student mentoring program. *Urban Education, 41,* 151-168.
58. Day-Vines, N. L., & Day-Hairston, B. O. (2005). Culturally congruent strategies for addressing the behavioral needs of urban, African American male adolescents. *Professional School Counseling, 8,* 236-243.
59. Givens, W. (2007, May 10). Preparing boys to be Men of Ardmore. *The Gazette,* Landover, MD.
60. Noguera, P. A. (2002). The trouble with black boys: The role and influence of environmental and cultural factors on the academic performance of African American males. Retrieved from http://www.inmotionmagazine.com

Made in the USA
San Bernardino, CA
20 September 2014